The 1529 Holy Week and Easter Sermons of Dr. Martin Luther

CONCORDIA ACADEMIC PRESS

SEMINARY EDITORIAL COMMITTEE
Charles Arand, Concordia Seminary, St. Louis, Missouri
Charles Gieschen, Concordia Theological Seminary, Ft. Wayne, Indiana
Paul Raabe, Concordia Seminary, St. Louis, Missouri
Peter Scaer, Concordia Theological Seminary, Ft. Wayne, Indiana
Detlev Schulz, Concordia Theological Seminary, Ft. Wayne, Indiana
James Voelz, Concordia Seminary, St. Louis, Missouri

Copyright © 1998 Concordia Publishing House
3558 S. Jefferson Avenue, St. Louis, MO 63118-3968
Manufactured in the United States of America

All rights reserved. No part of this publication may be reproduced, stored in a retrieval system, or transmitted, in any form or by any means, electronic, mechanical, photocopying, recording, or otherwise, without the prior written permission of Concordia Publishing House.

Library of Congress Cataloging-in-Publication Data.

Luther, Martin, 1483–1546
    [Predigten D. Martin Luthers auf Grund von Nachschriften Georg Rörers und Anton Lauterbachs. English]
    The 1529 Holy Week and Easter Sermons of Dr. Martin Luther/translated by Irving L. Sandberg; annotated with an introduction by Timothy J. Wengert.
        p.   cm.
    Includes bibliographical references.
       ISBN : 978-0-7586-4754-2
    1. Sermons, German—Translations into English. 2. Holy-Week sermons—Early works to 1800. 3. Easter—Sermons—Early works to 1800. 4. Lutheran Church—Sermons—Early works to 1800. I. Sandberg, Irving L., 1951– . II. Title.
BR332.S5   1999
252′.625—dc21   98-43556

The 1529 Holy Week and Easter Sermons of Dr. Martin Luther

Translated from
"Predigten D. Martin Luthers auf Grund von Nachschriften
Georg Rörers und Anton Lauterbachs"
edited by Georg Buchwald
(Gütersloh: Bertelsmann, 1925)

translated by Irving L. Sandberg
annotated with an introduction by Timothy J. Wengert

CONCORDIA PUBLISHING HOUSE • SAINT LOUIS

ACADEMIC PRESS

Contents

List of Illustrations 7

Abbreviations 9

Introduction 11

Palm Sunday Morning—March 21, 1529
    Matthew 21:1ff. and Confession 29

Palm Sunday Afternoon—March 21, 1529
    The Lord's Supper: On receiving Both Kinds 37

Monday Morning, Holy Week—March 22, 1529
    The Lord's Supper: On the Real Presence 45

Tuesday Morning, Holy Week—March 23, 1529
    The Lord's Supper: On Not Making the Sacrament a Work 55

Wednesday Morning, Holy Week—March 24, 1529
    The Lord's Supper: Received by Faith in the Word 63

Maundy Thursday Morning—March 25, 1529
    An Exhortation to Receive the Lord's Supper 71

Maundy Thursday Afternoon—March 25, 1529 The Passion:
    Anointing in Bethany, Last Supper, and Footwashing 81

Good Friday Morning—March 26, 1529
    The Passion: Gethsemane 89

Good Friday Afternoon—March 26, 1529
    The Passion: Trial and Crucifixion 97

Holy Saturday Morning—March 27, 1529
    The Passion: Words from the Cross 105

Holy Saturday Afternoon—March 27, 1529
    The Passion: Words from the Cross; Death and Burial   113

Easter Sunday Morning—March 28, 1529
    The Resurrection of Christ and Its Meaning   119

Easter Sunday Afternoon—March 28, 1529
    The Resurrection of Christ as Proclamation   129

Easter Monday Morning—March 29, 1529
    The Resurrection of Christ and Dying to the Law   137

Easter Monday Afternoon—March 29, 1529
    The Resurrected Christ Appears to Mary Magdalene
    (John 20:11–18)   143

Easter Tuesday Morning—March 30, 1529
    The Resurrected Christ Commissions the Disciples
    (John 20:19–20)   151

Easter Tuesday Afternoon—March 30, 1529
    The Purpose of Christ's Resurrection:
    Repentance and Forgiveness of Sin (Luke 24:45–47)   159

Easter Wednesday Morning—March 31, 1529
    The Resurrection of the Body (1 Corinthians 15:1ff.)   169

Illustrations

The title page illustration is also the title page for the first volume of the Jena edition of Luther's German works (Jena: Donatus Richtzenhain, 1560), depicting Luther and Duke John Frederick (until 1547 the elector of Saxony) adoring the Crucified. Courtesy Concordia Seminary Library, St. Louis, Missouri.

Illustrations on pages 11, 29, 37, 45, 55, 63, 71, 89, 97, 105, 113, and 159 are taken from Max Geisberg. *The German Single-Leaf Woodcut: 1500-1550.* Revised and edited by Walter L. Strauss (New York: Hacker Art Books, Inc., 1974), vols.1–4.

The Last Supper by Heinrich Vogtherr the Elder, c.1526. Hacker Art Books, p. 1373.   11

The Last Supper by Albrecht Dürer, 1523. Hacker Art Books, p. 695.   29

Agony in the Garden by Hans Weiditz, 1522. Hacker Art Books, p.1461.   37

Agony in the Garden by Lucas Cranach, the Elder, 1509. Hacker Art Books, p. 509.   45

Agony in the Garden by Lucas Cranach the Elder, 1502. Hacker Art Books, p. 523.   55

Christ before Caiaphas by Hans Schäufelein. Hacker Art Books, p. 984.   63

Pilate Washing His Hands by Hans Schäufelein. Hacker Art Books, p. 988.   71

Pilate Washing His Hands by Albrecht Dürer. *Behold the Christ* by Roland H. Bainton (New York: Harper & Row, 1974), p.138.   81

The Great Calvary from the Dürer School, c.1500. Hacker Art Books, p. 720.   89

Calvary by Lucas Cranach the Elder. Hacker Art Books, p. 525.   97

Christ on the Cross with the Virgin, the Magdalen, and St. John by an unidentified artist, c.1504. Hacker Art Books, p. 1564.   105

Descent from the Cross by Hans Baldung Grien, 1505. Hacker Art Books, p. 55.   113

The Resurrection by Albrecht Dürer, 1510. *Über das Bild des Auferstandenen und seinen Verlust in der Geschichte der deutschen Kunst* by Franz Joseph Klasen (Frankfurt am Main: Peter Lang, 1991), p. 269.   119

The Resurrection by Albrecht Dürer, 1509. Klasen, p. 237 (cf. above).   129

The Resurrection in *Sündenfall und Erlösung des Menschengeschlechtes* (München: G. Hirth's Verlag, 1888), p. 35.   137

The Gardener by Albrecht Dürer. Cf. Bainton (above p. 81), p.181.   143

The Resurrection of Christ (background: Samson with the Doors of Gaza) in Walter Eichberger/Henning Wendland, *Deutsche Bibeln vor Luther* (Hamburg: Friedrich Wittig Verlag, 1977), p. 133.   151

The Resurrection by Lucas Cranach the Elder, 1509. Hacker Art Books, p. 522.   159

Doubting Thomas by Albrecht Dürer in *The Life of Christ: Images from the Metropolitan Museum of Art*, compiled by Barbara Burn (New York: Charles Scribner's Sons, 1989), p. 89.   169

Abbreviations

BC	*The Book of Concord.* Edited by Theodore Tappert. Philadelphia: Fortress, 1959. (Numbers refer to paragraphs.)
Buchwald	Predigten D. Martin Luthers auf Grund von Nachschriften Georg Rörers und Anton Lauterbachs. Edited by Georg Buchwald, 2 vols. Gütersloh: Bertelsmann, 1925–26.
LBW	Lutheran Book of Worship. Minneapolis: Augsburg Publishing House, 1978.
Lenker	Sermons of Martin Luther. Edited and translated by John N. Lenker, 8 vols. Minneapolis, 1905–09; Reprint: Grand Rapids: Baker, 1989.
LuW	Lutheran Worship. St. Louis: Concordia, 1982.
LW	Luther's Works, American Edition. 55 vols. St. Louis and Philadelphia: Concordia and Fortress. 1955–86.
Mülhaupt	Luthers Evangelien-Auslegung. Edited by Erwin Mülhaupt, 5 vols. Göttingen: Vandenhoeck & Ruprecht, 1938–54.
NPNF	A Select Library of the Nicene and Post-Nicene Fathers of the Christian Church. Edited by Philip Schaaf. 28 vols. Reprint: Grand Rapids: Eerdmans, 1974–78.
PL	Patrologia cursus completus: Series Latina. 279 vols. Paris: Migne, 1859ff.
WA	Luthers Werke. Kritische Gesammtausgabe. Schriften. 60 vols. Weimar: H. Böhlau. 1883–1983.

Introduction

Martin Luther did not want to become a preacher. When as a monk he was assigned to preach at the Augustinian friary in Wittenberg, he co mplained he was not adequate to the task. Later, in 1514, when he was made assistant to the ailing pastor at St. Mary's parish church in Wittenberg, he also was filled with uncertainty. He could hardly have imagined then what an impact his preaching would have on his life and the church.[1]

The Reformation itself was more than anything else a result of Luther's preaching. The attack on indulgences began not with the 95 Theses on October 31, 1517, as is often imagined, but in sermons delivered earlier that year to his congregation. (Even the Theses themselves were motivated by the bad preaching of the indulgence sellers and the effect that preaching was having on Luther's parishioners.) Luther defended his public attacks by pointing not simply to his authority as professor of the Bible but also to his calling as preacher in Wittenberg—a calling so strongly felt, that in 1522 it caused him to abandon the relative security of the Wartburg Castle to return to Wittenberg to preach to his dear flock.[2] His most popular publications were not the carefully argued polemics or the dense biblical exegesis—intended for the most part for pastors and scholars—but his sermons and devotional literature. Two of his most important works, the Large and Small Catechisms, arose out of his own catechetical preaching. And many of his sermons were preserved in his Postil, a collection of sermons and commentaries on the appointed texts for the church year. The Postil in turn shaped the preaching and witness of generations of later Lutheran preachers.

In his career as an assistant at St. Mary's, stretching from 1514 until his death, Luther preached thousands of sermons. As his notoriety grew, students (including Philip Melanchthon in the early days) copied down his sermons and occasionally sold them to printers only too eager to fill Germany's bookstalls with works by the best-selling author of the day. Luther also sometimes took charge of publication himself. In the mid-1520s the Wittenberg city council actually hired someone to record Luther's words. For the rest of Luther's life, George Rörer, among others, transcribed many of Luther's sermons, including those translated below.

Although only about half of Luther's sermons have been preserved, nevertheless they account for the majority of volumes in the critical edition of his works. Besides the seven volumes translated into English in the American Edition of Luther's Works,[3] an earlier twentieth-century version of Luther's Postil edited by John Nicholas Lenker has also recently been reprinted. Excerpts from his Christmas and Easter preaching are also available in English.[4]

The following sermons, which comprise Luther's Holy Week and Easter preaching in 1529, show us Luther at the height of his expository power and demonstrate the depth of his pastoral concern. Not published during Luther's lifetime (with one exception), these sermons existed as notes from two or sometimes three separate sources, which recorded Luther's words in a mixture of German and Latin shorthand. They were first published in the critical edition of Luther's Works in 1904. Scholars soon recognized their usefulness for today's pastors and preachers. As a result, in 1925 Georg Buchwald published a reconstruction of sermons delivered between 1528 and 1532, based largely upon the Latin/German notes of Rörer.[5] His work was dedicated to the American Lutheran scholar and professor John Michael Reu, one of the most famous professors at Wartburg Seminary in Dubuque, Iowa, whose work on sixteenth-century Lutheran catechisms, including Luther's, is still unsurpassed. This translation is based largely upon Buchwald's work. However, after World War II Erwin Mülhaupt published much more extensive reconstructions that broadened Buchwald's material by relying on other notetakers than simply Rörer and by putting Luther's words into a more modern German. The present volume also uses this material to provide a fuller text.[6]

Like the work of both Buchwald and Mülhaupt, the sermons translated here are intended as preaching helps. Holy Week and Easter preaching still claims the energy of Christian pastors in our day. One resource they can now count on is the sermons of that reluctant, yet brilliant preacher of St. Mary's in Wittenberg. His insights into the biblical text and the human condition, into the Lord's Supper and the Passion and Resurrection of Christ, can still challenge and stimulate Christian proclamation today.

Luther's Situation in 1529

The best of times; the worst of times. Dickens' famous introduction to A Tale of Two Cities also describes the political and religious landscape in Luther's Wittenberg of 1529. In Electoral Saxony since 1527 teams of theologians, jurists, and court counselors had been crisscrossing the prince's territories in an extended visitation of the churches. "Dear God, what misery I beheld!" Luther exclaimed in the 1529 preface to the Small Catechism, as he reflected on his own brief experience as a visitor. Pastors were often underpaid or unpaid and untrained; parishioners had learned the fine art of abusing Christian freedom now that medieval laws governing religious life were no longer in force. Congregations were still unsettled as a result of the Peasants' Revolt of 1525. And the visitation itself, coming without permission from the regular bishops in league with Rome, had caused a political crisis in the Empire itself, leading eventually to the calling of the Imperial Diet in Augsburg and the presentation of the Augsburg Confession in 1530.

The challenges in Wittenberg were somewhat less daunting than in the rest of Saxony. The worship life had begun to change in 1521-22 with the earliest examples of lay communion in both kinds (bread and wine). After an initial period of unrest, in which theologians like Andrew Bodenstein von Karlstadt and Gabriel Zwilling called for the destruction of images and changes in the liturgy, Luther's own firm hand fixed a different course. Images remained; Latin was the language of liturgy, with German being slowly introduced after 1525; persons could commune in one or both kinds (an option that remained until 1540). In 1529 most all in Luther's congregation would have vividly recalled the differences between their former life "under the Pope" and their present one "in the Gospel," to use their terms for it. Enemies of Wittenberg and its rebel Augustinian friar continued to haunt the congregation. They included not only supporters of Rome but also of the deceased leaders of the Peasants' Revolt and the so-called sacramentarians, who denied Christ's presence in the Lord's Supper. Ignorance and the clinging to old traditions were also a concern. Opponents were not simply at a distance but came from the next town or the next duchy. Sermons during Holy Week gave Wittenberg's preachers a welcome opportunity to address the uncertainty their fellow citizens experienced, particularly regarding the Lord's Supper.

In 1529, however, the task of preaching fell completely on Luther's shoulders. That spring, Johannes Bugenhagen, the chief preacher at St. Mary's, was still away reforming the cities of Braunschweig and later Hamburg. This left Luther with the bulk of the preaching assignments. During Holy Week and the first week of Easter, eleven days in all, Luther preached eighteen sermons.[7] Of that number, the first dealt with Palm Sunday and included a lengthy exhortation to Confession and the following five with the Lord's Supper. The next eleven, preached from the afternoon of Maundy Thursday until the afternoon of Easter Tuesday, handled explicitly Jesus' death and resurrection. The final sermon, from Easter Wednesday, used Paul's comments about Christ's resurrection in 1 Corinthians 15 to investigate the question of the resurrection at the last day. Together they provide a glimpse into what Luther actually preached to his own congregation, how he perceived their need, and how he molded the Gospel to their capacities.

Sermons 1–6: Instructing the Simple in the Lord's Supper

In our day of religious ferment, it is understandable that pastors sometimes complain about the less-than-adequate religious training of their congregational members. Yet nothing can compare to the upheaval and ignorance in Luther's day. Then, all the adults had experienced a very different approach to private confession of sin, called the Sacrament of Penance, and to the Lord's Supper. Since so many of Luther's congregants still held to the tradition of confessing and communing during Holy Week and Easter, he seized the opportunity to instruct them in these matters. So successful were these sermons that they formed the basis for his remarks on both subjects in the Large Catechism, which he was writing at precisely this time.[8]

In the lone sermon on Confession, Luther explored new territory for an evangelical preacher, as he had to avoid both the "slaughter of souls" of past church rules that demanded yearly confession and the abuse of freedom that kept people away from private confession altogether. He did this by focusing on the Word of absolution, "God's work," in which sins are actually forgiven and burdens lifted from the weak. Luther realized that what will bring people to confession is the same thing that will bring a beggar to the place where they are handing out free coats: the gift itself and our recognized need. (He revisited these very arguments on Thursday morning, when he exhorted his people to receive the Lord's Supper.)

Luther placed his remarks on the Lord's Supper in a framework that might surprise twentieth-century ears. He realized that, according to Wittenberg's practice, the good burghers of Wittenberg would have heard about the Supper at least four times a year, during the regular sermons on the catechism. Nonetheless, he preached on it extensively "for God's Word and work in the world are received in such a way that Satan does not gladly allow it to remain in its true use and essence."[9] Catechetical instruction and doctrinal sermons were for Luther a matter not of informing the interested but of defending those under attack. The stakes were high: God's Word always rouses Satan's ire, especially in something as comforting as the Lord's Supper.

Luther's sermons dealt with a variety of issues, but all under the aegis of the power and authority of God's Word. In the first he covered the institution of the meal and the issue of communion in two kinds. Here the question revolved around Christ's command to "Do this!" Addressing specifically the argument that because the church had accepted the Gospel it had authority to change such matters as communion in both kinds, Luther insisted that our accepting an authority puts us under it, not above it. Moreover, since according to the text the Supper was given to the "disciples" and since disciples included even women, as the reference to Tabitha in Acts 9 demonstrated, the command to drink included all believers, not just priests.

If the devil was trying to steal part of the sacrament from believers in Roman Catholic practice, he also attempted to steal the whole thing from them in the sacramentarians' claim that Christ was not present in the bread and wine. Again Luther pitted the authority of God's Word against the reasonable argument that if Christ is in heaven he cannot be in the bread. "You must put out the eyes of reason and toss them into the pit of hell. Instead you must let God's Word be true and cling to it with closed eyes and ears."[10] To Luther this challenge to the plain words in Christ's institution of the Supper smacked of Satan's trickery, which had undermined Adam and Eve's trust in God with a single question: "But why?"

Tuesday's sermon turned from the sacramentarians' challenge back to the Roman argument that the mass is a sacrifice. If the former distrusted Christ's word, "This is my Body," the latter ran roughshod over the phrase "given for you." This simple, two-fold promise ("my body" and "given for you") revealed for Luther that the benefits of the Lord's Supper and, thus, the proper preparation for receiving it consisted in faith alone. While "the devil and all the papists have the first faith" (in Christ's presence), they cannot believe the second, that the Sacrament is "for you."[11] As in the Large Catechism itself, a subtle shift occurred in Luther's language: again and again he called the Supper a treasure.

The centrality of Christ's command and promise then served as the basis for Luther's exhortation to Holy Communion. As in the case of Confession, people had begun to neglect the Sacrament once the regulation regarding yearly communion had been lifted. Luther was at his pastoral best as he used both the command of Christ, the treasure in the Supper, and his hearers' desperate need to bring people to the Lord's Table. He had experienced their weakness himself; he knew the tricks of Satan firsthand; he had no ecclesiastical authority only the power of the Word to bring his people to their senses. This final sermon, like the equivalent passage in the Large Catechism, defined a radically evangelical approach to inactive, sleeping Christians, from which today's pastors and congregations may also learn a thing or two.

Sermons 7–18: Christ's Death and Resurrection for the Simple

Among the songs Luther wrote for Johann Walther's "Spiritual Song Booklet" of 1524, the first evangelical hymnal, was "Christ lag in Todesbanden" ("Christ Jesus Lay in Death's Strong Bands").[12] This hymn contains almost all that Luther had to say about Christ's death and resurrection. It reads in part

> It was a strange and dreadful strife
> When life and death contended;
> The victory remained with life,
> The reign of death was ended.
> Holy Scripture plainly says
> That death is swallowed up by death,
> Its sting is lost forever. Hallelujah!
>
> Here the true Paschal Lamb we see,
> Whom God so freely gave us;
> He died on the accursed tree—
> So strong His love to save us.
> See, his blood now marks our door;
> Faith points to it; death passes o'er,
> And Satan cannot harm us. Hallelujah!
>
> Then let us feast this Easter Day
> On Christ, the bread of heaven;
> The Word of grace has purged away
> The old and evil leaven.
> Christ alone our souls will feed;
> He is our meat and drink indeed;
> Faith lives upon no other! Hallelujah!

Here Luther portrayed Christ as victor, but in a "strange and dreadful" (*wunderlich*) strife; he emphasized the clarity of the Scripture and the centrality of Christ's death in our place, to which faith points in the face of the devil's attacks; here the Christian sings that Christ alone saves and, thus, works are excluded.[13]

In fact, this song reveals that for Luther the proclamation of the death and resurrection of Jesus Christ creates faith by eliminating all false objects of our trust (such as works, reason, free choice) and by leaving us with the Righteous One alone whose victorious rising left our sins in his grave. To preach Christ crucified is to apply the words from the cross to us directly so that faith is born; to preach Christ raised is to apply his triumph over death, witnessed by the women and disciples in their weakness, to us in our weakness.

Luther had published comments on Christ's death and resurrection earlier in his career as well. In the Spring of 1519, while in the midst of the battle with Rome and preparations for the Leipzig debates with his life-long opponent, John Eck, Martin Luther published a tract entitled "Sermon on Looking at Christ's Suffering," usually translated as "A Meditation on Christ's Passion."[14] This "sermon" (a word used here as a technical term for an essay on a theme) most likely began in Luther's own preaching on Christ's death during the services on Good Friday in the same year. It was included by him in the Lenten postil (*Fastenpostil*), published in 1525.

To appreciate the uniqueness of Luther's comments on Christ's death, we need to remember what the alternatives were in his day. In 1519 he wrote: "Some people meditate on Christ's passion by venting their anger on the Jews. ... That might well be a meditation on the wickedness of Judas and the Jews, but not on the sufferings of Christ."[15] In 1529 he criticized those who miss the point of the story and only used it for "moving old women to tears and even pointing out the evil of the Jews."[16] Tears or hatred of Jews missed the point. "Rather one should consider the prophecies of the holy prophets, especially Isaiah, that the Passion of Christ is a punishment for our sins."[17] He even went so far as to say that since the word "Jew" meant "one who confesses," then those who praise Christ were true Jews.[18]

In fact, both approaches (tears and hatred) were current in the late-medieval church. On the one hand, the Passion was depicted with startling reality—in late-medieval paintings blood gushes everywhere—in order to cause the hearers to feel pity for Christ and sorrow for their sins and thus to prepare them for penance and making satisfaction for their sins through their own suffering. By 1529 such an approach was part of the audience's past. They used to hear that their own suffering and patience took away sin. To continue to combat this notion, Luther stressed that "all human suffering in a heap" could not take away one sin and that there was therefore an infinite difference between Christ's suffering and ours. If suffering made us godly, the devil would be the godliest of all.[19]

On the other hand, medieval preaching attacked the Jews and was sometimes the immediate cause for the customary Holy Week pogroms. Luther's preaching brought both approaches to a halt. However despicable his tract against the Jews, written in old-age, was,[20] in fact Luther at one blow removed preaching against the Jews during Holy Week from evangelical pulpits. Holy Week sermons published by Lutherans during the sixteenth century rarely mention the Jews. Descriptions of the horrors of suffering also disappeared. Luther even took pains to point out in 1529 that the actual crucifixion was depicted by only a single verse in all the gospels, because the evangelists had more important things on which to focus!

In the same sermon from 1519 Luther also eliminated contemplation (which he views as merely a way "to seek [one's] own advantage"), feeling pity, and simply hearing the story recited, as if it were effective *ex opere operato*.[21] Instead Luther insisted that

> they contemplate Christ's passion aright who view it with a terror-stricken heart and a despairing conscience. ... And if you seriously consider that it is God's very own Son ... who suffers, you will be terrified indeed. The more you think about it, the more intensely will you be frightened. [22]

Luther continued, "You must get this through your head and not doubt that you are the one who is torturing Christ thus, for your sins have surely wrought this."[23] Now it becomes clear why Luther eliminated preaching against the Jews: they did not do it, we did. It was worse than being implicated as the mastermind in the death of the child of a king.

> You should be terrified even more by the meditation on Christ's passion. For the evildoers, the Jews, whom God has judged and driven out, were only the servants of your sin; you are actually the one[s] who, as we said, by [your] sin killed and crucified God's Son.[24]

What the pope first declared after Vatican II, namely, that the Jews were not to blame for Christ's death, Luther had already proclaimed in 1519 and 1529 and had passed on to his theological heirs, so that Johann Heermann could write 100 years later, "Who was the guilty? Who brought this upon thee? Alas, my treason, Jesus, hath undone thee. 'Twas I, Lord Jesus, I it was denied thee; I crucified thee."[25]

Luther also insisted that the preaching of the cross does something to us. It is not information to contemplate or drama to titillate. It is the murder of God's Son and the unmasking of the murderers, us. And that unmasking is not accomplished by our will, effort, work or contemplative skill, it is granted only by God, when he strangles the old creature.

Because this strangling is in God's hands, not ours, it implied for Luther the heart of the theology of the cross, which is not a theory about the cross or how it works but the "revelation of God under the form of opposites," or to put it in modern language, "God revealed hidden in the last place we would ever look." Thus, some who never think about Christ's passion are nevertheless crushed by evil, while others look at Christ's passion but never get an inkling of the evil in their lives. "For [the former] the passion of Christ is hidden and genuine, while for [the latter] it is only unreal and misleading. In that way God often reverses matters. ..."[26]

Precisely for these crushed and strangled ones Luther had good news: the resurrection is the only solution for the sinner's predicament. Medieval preaching of the cross intended to lead a person to seek the Sacrament of Penance and to begin or continue the life of a penitent, working out through one's deeds satisfaction of the temporal punishment for sin. Thus, the sacramental system became the solution to the sinner's dilemma posed by Christ's death. Luther, by rejecting the entire penitential system of the church, returned to the patristic focus on the resurrection. If our sin killed Christ, then it is buried with Christ. But he rises without that sin and becomes, as Luther said elsewhere, the sin of sin and death of death. Thus, the risen Christ is precisely the Righteous One without sin, to whom we cling by faith alone.

On this transfer of our sin to Christ we must stake everything. "The more your conscience torments you, the more tenaciously must you cling to [verses in the Bible that cast our sins on Christ]." If we look instead to our contrition or penitence, Luther warned, the result will overwhelm us and sin will remain with us. "But if we behold it resting on Christ and overcome by his resurrection, and then boldly believe this, even it [sin] is dead and nullified. Sin cannot remain on Christ, since it is swallowed up by his resurrection."[27] Luther's insistence that our sin put Christ on the cross, far from becoming "worm theology" or a method by which to manipulate people into feeling guilty, was simply the cutting edge of the Good News of the resurrection. God will not allow your evil deeds, your rebellion, to have the last word.

As a consequence of this new focus on the resurrection, faith alone became the center of the Christian's relation to God. That is, the proclamation of Christ's death and resurrection itself, not something that happened behind the scenes or some example or feeling it may evoke, but the proclamation itself spells death and resurrection to the rebellious children of Adam and Eve. It destroys all our claims to "work out" our relation to God and replaces them with faith alone. Here is Christ for you; here is forgiveness for your sin; here in the death of Christ perpetrated by you and in the resurrection effected by God. From that proclamation faith is born. And, as if to anticipate the work-happy Christians of our own time who make faith a religious decision of ours, Luther refused to turn faith into a work. He concluded:

> If ... you cannot believe, you must entreat God for faith. This too rests entirely in the hands of God. What we said about suffering also applies here, namely, that sometimes faith is granted openly, sometimes in secret.[28]

At the same time, Luther urged Christians who have doubts not to remain fixed on the terror of Christ's death but on the kindness and love of Christ, behind which beats the loving heart of God. Again the theology of the cross rescued Luther and his readers from contemplating God's terrifying choices.

> We know God aright when we grasp him not in his might or wisdom (for then he proves terrifying), but in his kindness and love. There faith and confidence are able to exist, and then [the person] is truly born anew in God.[29]

Only after having worked the death and resurrection of Christ on his hearers, did Luther suggest that for the "heart firm in Christ" the cross could become a pattern for one's entire life.

In 1529 Luther worked out in more detail the basic contours of his thought outlined in 1519. In the first sermons on the Passion and the Resurrection (Maundy Thursday afternoon and Easter Sunday morning) Luther gave a general introduction to the topics. He then followed that with a verse-by-verse approach to recount the story, as he himself admitted, for the sake of the simple, "who do not know what happened on this day."[30]

One of the best examples of Luther's simple approach to Christ's death and resurrection came in his sermon devoted to the exchange between Jesus and the thief on the cross. For Luther there was no better example of comfort in the entire Bible than the thief's prayer, "Jesus, remember me." The thief is the first believer, the true abbot. He has a heart larger than heaven and earth. He must have had purified eyes to see Christ as savior. The exchange between Christ and the thief outlined Christ's work with us. "This is the Gospel, that one does not become a Christian through one's works, but through Christ. This is so fine a faith that it is a joy."[31]

Although Luther focused on the story, he had a different approach than the Passionalia of the time—booklets that depicted the mocking of Christ in gruesome detail. While explicitly not rejecting such depictions, he insisted that the real point was that the Gospel of Christ's coming kingdom is always treated with mockery and at the same time creates faith.

Luther's 1529 sermons discover the tension, paradox and movement from death to resurrection—central to Luther's experience of God's Word—in the text, its characters and Christ's words. For example, Luther could reflect on the inscription over the cross, that to this day others see Christ as a revolutionary but believers confess Christ as king. Luther's own opponents also infiltrated the story and helped him define for his hearers types of unbelief. Other preachers of the passion who did not understand it were in the next duchy or the monastery[32] and included "Enthusiasts," Anabaptists, and revolutionaries.[33]

Luther also attacked what even today is still the most prevalent way to view Christ's death: as an example. As Christ suffered for [original] sin, so we must suffer for our daily sin, the theory went. What he labeled monastic theology and idolatry (the worship of our suffering) Luther rejected out-of-hand as contradicting what for him was the central text for the crucifixion: "Here is the Lamb of God who takes away the sin of the world." No wonder Lucas Cranach in his Wittenberg altar depicted Luther in the pulpit, like John the Baptist, pointing to the crucified Christ for his hearers. Perhaps the artist could still hear Luther saying: "Do not mix your suffering with Christ's suffering but separate them from one another like heaven from earth or gold from manure."[34]

To be sure, Luther sometimes saw the text as an example for us. Christ's weakness at Gethsemane is "an example meant to comfort us" in our own weakness and in our dealing with the weakness of others.[35] At the same time it effects something else. "When you see Christ weak, think 'it is your sins.'" But Luther hastened to add, "But this is by far the hardest thing of all; it doesn't fit our expectations. How can reason believe it?"[36] These words catch the magnitude of the claim made by the cross and the difficulty of comprehending it by faith. Nonetheless, that is the heart of the message of the passion. After noting that the passion begins in the Garden because the Fall took place in one, Luther went on to say:

> Take careful notice of Christ's stripes and wounds, for they are our sins. And read inscribed on the bonds, chains, and blows: mine, mine, my sins! so that we preserve ourselves from boasting in our own suffering.[37]

Luther did from time to time discuss difficulties in the text with his congregation, but usually, as in the case of how many times Christ was questioned by the Sanhedrin, he concluded by returning to the main point: he suffered for me, "as if this was written over [his humiliation]: My sin!"[38] Johann Heermann captured this in his hymn, "Ah, Holy Jesus": "For me, kind Jesus, was thine incarnation, thy mortal sorrow, and thy life's oblation; thy death of anguish and thy bitter Passion, for my salvation."[39] And Paul Gerhardt penned, "Thy grief and bitter passion were all for sinners' gain; mine, mine was the transgression, but thine the deadly pain."[40]

Luther took special pains to explain some of Christ's words from the cross, especially those in Luke. It was the words, "Father, forgive them," that show Christ is truly our high priest, clothed in obedience to the Father, offering his own blood, and praying for us. "Our cowls and tonsures won't help. The prayer of the High Priest must help."[41]

Luther steadfastly refused to turn faith into a human virtue and, unlike Enthusiasts in our day and his who insist on the security of their faith and boast in it, Luther took a completely different tack. For him, faith coexisted with doubt and uncertainty. Contrasting the security of those mocking Christ to the agony of the Crucified, he said:

> We believe in Christ, but sometimes he leaves us so alone, as if there were no God who accepts us, and we appear so forsaken, that they can make a mockery and game from it. This grieves Christians when they see in themselves such struggle and fear, but on the other side such strengths.[42]

The role of the devil was also heightened in these sermons. Thus, Luther depicted all the devil's rage, normally reserved for us, being heaped upon Christ. This means that when the devil hears the name Jesus Christ spoken with true faith he is defeated, "as if thunderstruck."[43] Here and elsewhere the strains of "A Mighty Fortress," first published in 1528 or 1529, echo throughout Luther's sermons. This became even clearer in the sermons on the resurrection.

Among the Easter sermons, Luther's first on Easter morning introduced the entire subject. Again he worried about misinterpretations of the resurrection, especially by those who think of it as just another story painted on the wall. He referred his hearers instead to the Easter sequence that he included in Wittenberg's hymnals: "Christ is arisen from the grave's dark prison. So let our joy rise full and free; Christ our comfort true will be."[44] Thus on Easter you must not simply see how the Resurrection occurred, but that it occurred *for you*. Again, it is faith alone that drives the sermon. It is not enough to say, Christ is a king and a savior, but "He is *my* Savior and *my* king."[45]

Here again is the language of "A Mighty Fortress," which names Jesus Christ the "*rechter Mann*," or true champion. "But when you place your faith in his works, then he is such a champion, giant, and hero, who had arrayed against him the gates of hell, all devils with their cunning, and death with all its powers."[46] Thus, one cannot simply look at the story, or tell it, because there is no comfort there. Instead, one must open the eyes of the heart. Then one sees that it is my sin and death that put Jesus in the grave and that when he arose he left them there. On the cross my sins crush Christ, but as soon as they thought they had defeated him, "the Lion tears himself away from sin, death, hell and the jaws of the devil and rips them to shreds with his teeth."[47]

Any time a sermon comes along and says, "You've sinned, therefore you must do thus and so," it is the devil's sermon and makes a mockery of God and the resurrection. Instead, Luther advised his congregation, to send the devil to Christ, on whom our sins were laid, and to fix our gaze on the resurrected Christ, who left them buried in the grave.[48]

The devil wants to rip this picture from our hearts. So when a Christian undergoes any struggle [Anfechtung], he or she should say that this does not matter to me for I have no sins; Christ has them all. ... He took them on himself on the cross and buried them. But now he lives and is risen."[49] Immediately Luther returned to an old theme. "And yet it is true: I am a sinner and I am not one." If I say I am not a sinner, then Christ didn't die for me. If I am a sinner only in myself, then I am lost.

> If I am in myself a condemned sinner but go outside myself and into Christ, then I am not one. Christians from their own standpoint are a Judas, a Caiaphas, a Pilate and find themselves condemned. But there is another Person, who took my sins upon himself. On Good Friday they are all laid around his neck. But on Easter I look at him and then he has none. ... [F]or where there is no sin there is righteousness and life.[50]

The other side to Luther's view of the Easter story was the weakness of the human witnesses: the apostles and women alike. In telling the story of the angel's appearance to the women, Luther emphasizes the strength of the angels and their message and points out that from the very beginning of the resurrection nothing happens apart from the external Word. In contrast to the Enthusiasts who looked for Christ in their own spiritual exercises, it was the spoken, external Gospel itself that served as Christ's "Wagon."

This strong word Luther contrasted to the weakness of the women. Yet, given our own peculiar sensitivities, it would be a mistake to chalk this up to misogyny at all. Luther found no comfort in eggheads and kings, that is, the powerful who do not understand the Gospel. The angels came to the weakest. The text itself indicated to Luther just how foolish they were: buying spices and walking to the tomb before they had considered the problem of the stone. His point was not to mock the women but to identify with them.[51]

And when Christ told Mary Magdalene to "tell my brothers," Luther could not say enough about the tremendous promise he heard there. He encouraged his hearers to write these words in golden letters, in capital letters: that the one who had no brothers wants to share the inheritance he has from the Father with us. In the world, one would just as soon see all one's brothers dead, so he could inherit alone. But Christ defies the world and our reason, and calls us brothers. "Whoever can believe [Christ is their brother] is a Christian."[52]

What characterized Luther's sermons in 1529? First, as was characteristic of all Luther's preaching, he single-mindedly focused on the "main point" of the text: in the case of the crucifixion that we killed Christ by our sins; in the case of the resurrection that Christ rose for me so that sin, death and the devil are defeated. Other issues and methods, whether concern over history or the use of allegory, finally had to bow to the main point. Second, Luther did not treat the main point as simply a doctrine to be learned or a story to be recited, but as an event to be experienced. His use of direct address, paraphrase and exaggeration, as well as his identification of the characters with his own situation, served to crucify and raise his hearers, so that they experience Christ's suffering, death and resurrection. Thus terms like "Law and Gospel" cannot be used in a formalized manner to divide Luther's sermons or to describe his approach. Instead one only sees Law and Gospel at work, effecting both death, by confronting the hearer with his or her complicity in the cross, and resurrection, by proclaiming the strong word of the resurrection and forgiveness to the weak.[53]

It is our hope that the same lively Word that worked on Luther's hearers might once again be let loose in the church today.

Timothy J. Wengert
Irving L. Sandberg
Ash Wednesday, 1997

Endnotes

[1] For more on Luther as preacher, see Fred W. Meuser, Luther the Preacher (Minneapolis: Augsburg, 1983).

[2] Upon his return he delivered eight sermons in a week to explain the relation between faith and church practice and to defuse the unrest and iconoclasm in the city. See LW 51:69–100.

[3] Volumes 21–24, 30, 51–52.

[4] *The Martin Luther Christmas Book: With Celebrated Woodcuts by His Contemporaries*, trans. Roland H. Bainton (Philadelphia: Fortress, n.d.) and *The Martin Luther Easter Book*, trans. Roland H. Bainton (Philadelphia: Fortress, 1983). Also, *Sermons of Martin Luther* (House Postil), trans. Eugene Klug, 3 vols. (Grand Rapids: Baker, 1996).

[5] Buchwald, 1:272–396.

[6] Mülhaupt, 5:75–100, 232–61, 348–85. In a few instances, the original notes in WA 29:132–381 have also been consulted.

[7] All are included in Buchwald's work with the exception of the sermon for Easter Tuesday morning, for which Mülhaupt's reconstruction has been used.

[8] BC, 337–461.

[9] See below, p. 48.

[10] Ibid, p. 64.

[11] Ibid, p. 96.

[12] LBW 134, LuW 123. See also LW 53:255–57.

[13] Luther's other Easter hymn, written in 1528 or 1529 is "A Mighty Fortress" (LBW 229; LuW 297).

[14] LW 42:5–14.

[15] LW 42:7.

[16] See below, p. 132.

[17] Ibid.

[18] Ibid, p. 158.

[19] Ibid, p. 134.

[20] *On the Jews and Their Lies*, 1543 (LW 47:121–306).

[21] By the mere performance of the act. LW 42:7f.

[22] LW 42:8f.

[23] LW 42:9. He referred to Peter's Pentecost sermon in Acts 2.

[24] LW 42:10.

[25] LBW 123.

[26] LW 42:11f.

[27] LW 42:12.

[28] LW 42:13.

[29] Ibid.

[30] See below, p. 193. See also his Good Friday afternoon sermon on the arrest of Jesus, p. 145.

[31] Ibid, p. 165.
[32] Especially John Cochlaeus, the chief theological advisor to Duke George of Saxony.
[33] See below, pp. 138 and 141.
[34] Ibid, p. 137.
[35] Ibid, p. 140.
[36] Ibid.
[37] Ibid, p. 142.
[38] Ibid, p. 148.
[39] LBW 123. Heermann lived from 1585 to 1647.
[40] LBW 117. Gerhardt lived from 1607 to 1676. These two hymns mark a quite different, Lutheran piety and contrast sharply, for example, to the contemporaneous hymn of the Anglican Puritan, Samuel Crossman (c. 1624–1683), "My Song Is Love Unknown" (LBW 94; LuW 91), where the perpetrators of Christ's death are someone else. ("They" kill "my dear Lord.")
[41] See below, p. 153.
[42] Ibid, p. 159.
[43] Ibid, p. 161.
[44] LBW 136; with different words LuW 124.
[45] See below, p. 184.
[46] Ibid.
[47] Ibid, p. 185.
[48] Ibid, p. 186.
[49] Ibid, p. 189.
[50] Ibid, p. 189f.
[51] Ibid, p. 198f.
[52] Ibid, p. 224.
[53] Luther also could interpret the suffering of Christ in the light of our cross and trials. See LW 51:195–208 for a Holy Saturday sermon he preached at the Castle Coburg, just before Elector John and his entourage left for Augsburg in 1530.

Palm Sunday Morning
March 21, 1529
Matthew 21:1ff. and Confession

You last heard this Gospel on the first Sunday in Advent.[1] For this reason it is not necessary to preach on it at length. We will deal with the text briefly: You heard that this Gospel describes Christ's entry into Jerusalem and the events that happened on that day. The Lord was in Bethany at the home of his beloved hostess Martha and dined there, and Mary anointed him. On the following day early in the morning he sent two disciples to fetch a donkey, and then he went to Jerusalem. But there was a great multitude of people who had come to the feast from all over, and everyone sought to see him. For this reason the priests were angry with the Lord.

But the Lord was honored in that when the people heard he was coming from Bethany, everyone flocked to him with all their might, as the people were in the habit of doing, desiring to see him. The disciples were moved to shout out loud, and the people added their cheers in the belief that he would be king. Others scattered branches on the way, as is done when a king approaches. And the children sang Hosanna in the temple. But the priests were angry and unwilling to put up with it. The Lord answered them, "Have you never read, 'Out of the mouths of infants and nursing babies you have prepared praise for yourself'?" [Matthew 21:16].

But this wonderful joy ended in this way: After he had preached the entire day, there was no one who would give him lodging, as Mark 11:11 says, Jesus "looked around at everything," to see whether there was anyone who would allow him to spend the night in his house. For the great rulers were angry. Therefore the people forgot about their dear king quite quickly when they saw he had not put on a show and was not about to change his tune. These are the events of this day. The main point of this Gospel you have heard in Advent.[2]

The other part in the Gospel is the fruit of faith that follows from this saying: "Look, your king is coming to you" [Matthew 21:5] and is demonstrated in the words: "Hosanna to the Son of David!" [Matthew 21:9] and, as Mark 11:10 describes, "Blessed is the coming kingdom of our ancestor David! Hosanna in the highest heaven!" This is the faith that bears all kinds of fruits, namely, so that this cry may result: "Hosanna to the Son of David!" This is a true, spiritual Christian song that no one except Christians sing.

Hosanna is not understood by many and has been made into a woman's name. Osanna is not a woman's name; Suzanna is. *Hosia* means please help, give good fortune, salvation, victory, so that the Lord may rule, may triumph,[3] as we see in the Psalm Confitemini:[4] "Save us, O Lord! O Lord, give us success! Blessed is the one who comes in the name of the Lord!" (Psalm 118:25). Hosanna is a song and praise that is in every Christian heart. For this is our worship that we praise the blessing which is given to us without payment.

But now there are few who can sing the song that the children sang. It is only a short word, but it is an art to sing it from a true heart. Indeed people who stand on their works do not sing this song. They do not wish good fortune and victory to Christ, but rather to themselves. *Hosia* means the same thing as 'Long live the King!', just as people call out in Italy, '*Vive Papa!*' 'Long live the Pope!' But people who believe they are saved through their merits praise their own works. But the righteous praise Christ and not their works. Indeed Christ needs neither a sacrifice in a temple nor calves and cows, but indicates instead that we may give such help to the poor, as he says in Matthew 25:35ff. He loves to hear *Hosia*.

Na, which indicates a sighing and longing, means in Hebrew "O do help,"[5] as in those who wish that all human doctrines would collapse in a heap and would give room to the gospel, so that it might be recognized. Such people sing Hosanna properly. This is the fruit of faith and the highest work that follows immediately from the recognition of the Gospel, namely, that the gospel triumphs.

Easter is drawing near. It is necessary to instruct you about the sacrament of the Lord's Supper and then also about the suffering and the resurrection of the Lord. For this reason I will deal with the portions that are necessary so that for three days I can preach about the sacrament. But I have already urged you[6] to divide yourselves up, so that the servants of the church can get to everyone. For now just four persons are present to hear confession.[7] Previously we had two cloisters and the priests in the rectory.

Now we propose to preach on confession and on the sacrament.[8]

Dear friends, you have learned that confession should be voluntary. Some among you have learned this freedom all too well according to the flesh, and, as a result, give all freedom to the flesh and seek nothing in the gospel but a fleshly certainty. We learn quite easily where the Gospel benefits us. I have no desire to preach to swine but say to them who mistake the Gospel for freedom of the flesh that they should be compelled to do everything again that the pope had imposed on them. For whoever is not willing to submit to hearing the Gospel is not worthy to have it. I do not preach to such people who would be free according to the flesh.

They have heard that the Gospel has freed us from the confession which the pope had imposed on us. There was no more difficult burden in Christianity, for we were compelled to a confession that we did not gladly make. Thus we were weighed down with recounting all kinds of sins, so that no one was able to confess purely enough. We also had not been taught what confession is—how it must be sweet for us and in what it really consists—but we were forced to it like swine. But now you are no longer forced to it like the pope forced us with threats of damnation. For such people the pope is still rightly the Lord God's devil. He laid on us the burden of God's curse. But now you are no longer forced to it with the loss of salvation.[9] Secondly, you are no longer compelled to enumerate all the sins which you have committed throughout the year.[10] Thirdly, you receive a comfort in confession and know what it is, namely, not a troublesome and bitter thing but rather sugar, honey and comfort.

Confession consists of these two parts. The first, that I grieve over my sins and desire the refreshment of my soul, is my work. But the other part, that the priest speaks simply an absolution, is God's work. That makes the confession comforting. Previously the people had been directed to enumerate all their sins, in short, to focus on all their works. The teaching of the righteous is easy as Solomon says (Proverbs 14:6), but the foolish have torment, work, and it is bitter for them. Thus it was with confession, but nothing was never said of the best part, namely, the absolution. My work—the least important part, which comes from us—was praised; nothing was said of the other—the most important part—which is God's. But do not think that through this work of confession I will become righteous; on the contrary, the best part rests in the priest's mouth. For this reason it is important that you come for the comforting word that is entrusted to the priest.

Thus one may not force Christianity on you with commandments, but if you want to be a Christian or already are one, then come for the comfort! By the fact that we say that the Word and absolution are the greatest treasure in the priest's mouth, we have put away fully the pope's law and tyranny. For we say: all who want to purify themselves with their works and confession, let them not approach! But I, on the contrary, will advise you to confess your sins and declare your need, not in order to reckon this as a work, but so that you may hear what the priest has to say to you. You should come for the Word. For that is why the priest is present, to speak the Word to you and stand you back on your feet.

This is what you should consider, what should urge you on, that you act like a poor beggar who knows that somewhere cloth for coats is being handed out. It is not necessary to force him, but he comes of himself. Now if you said, "All beggars must go in there, there and no place else," and failed to mention the blessing, they would become so hostile at being compelled, that they would not want to go there at all. This is what the pope did; he did not show us the treasure. For this reason no one ever went gladly to confession. Now we make the mistake of not seeing how poor and wretched we are. But if you are mired in your sins, then go and get the abundant handouts! But those who do not come and confess are not Christians. For this reason, do not despise confession, even though we force no one to it. But if you are a Christian, then there is no need of my compulsion. You will come voluntarily that I may hear your confession.

But if any are so proud and want to go to the sacrament without confession, it should not be offered to them because they despise what no Christian despises.[11] But if they recognize their sin and desire the sacrament but refuse to go to confession, that would be the same as if one wanted to go to the sacrament but did not want to hear the Gospel. We dare not give the sacrament to swine but only to Christians. But if you are a Christian, then I need not force you to listen to the sermon, but your heart will compel you to force me to preach. Previously the pope had forced you to listen to the sermon. It was the same with confession. Formerly the pope forced you to confess; but now you should force me to hear your confession. For this reason whenever we admonish you to go to confession, we admonish you to become a Christian. If this is the case, then you will come in the proper way.

Some are so vulgar that they acknowledge no sin whatsoever and say to the deacon, "Give me absolution." To be sure, I have said it is impossible to enumerate all sins. But still you must say, "I have sinned in many ways; I have cursed, etc."[12] What most compels your conscience to confess, that you shall say. If the priest should absolve you of sins, then there also must be sin there. If you are a Christian, then your heart will teach you to confess. For if I have something that presses on my conscience, then I have no comfort until I hear someone say to me, "It is forgiven." This is what Christians do. But whoever will not do it belongs under the papacy. If you want to do nothing more than show yourself to the priest, stay at home.

Indeed I have said that people should come to confession on their own and look at the comfort and the treasure and God's Word that they hear in confession. If they do not want that, then let them stay home! However, many among you jump at the chance for comfort in order to hear the Word of God, as it is written in Psalm 42:1: "As a deer longs for flowing streams, so my soul longs for you, O God." These need not be compelled, but they come and compel us to hear their confession. Whoever is not of this sort, whoever needs no confession and stays away from it, we do not force such people to come to confession. It is the same as if someone would force me to expound the Psalter. Thus the laws and the compulsion are not on our side, but on theirs.[13]

But should the absolution depend on my holiness? No, instead say this: I confess what oppresses me in this hour, what I lack makes no difference. The absolution, which reads, "I proclaim to you peace," does not fail me.[14] For at that moment a penitent should forget what he or she has done and be carried away with this absolution and say: Whatever I may lack here and there, the saying which the priest has spoken over me is God's Word. This is as clear and plain as if Christ himself had said it, as in John 8:11, "Go and sin no more." As this absolution was comforting to the woman, so you should set your comfort in the word that the priest says to you. It is no other word than God's Word. Christ has commanded us to speak it.

Confession contains such a noble thing. I would not give up confession for all the riches in the world, even if all leaves and grains of sand were gold. And save for the sacrament, I know of no greater treasure and comfort than confession. Whoever does not know this comfort is not worthy to confess; let them go rather to the episcopal adjudicator[15] and confess without absolution. We must not look to our work but to the treasure, which we hear from the priest's mouth, which makes us go gladly and force the priests and not vice versa. If I want to hear it gladly, then I would have to become a beggar so that clothing could be given to me. But because we do not want to go to confession, the pastors force us to it. But now we pastors would love it, if we were forced by those confessing, as it is written in Matthew 11:12, "The kingdom of God has suffered violence and the violent take it by force." Those who do not yet feel this, let them ask God to have a desire for the fresh brook of divine comfort.

This is said briefly about the voluntary confession of Christians about which we preach. The confession which the pope has laid on us is a forced thing and thereby obscures the main part, which is the absolution. On the other hand, our confession is not coerced.

Besides auricular confession, there are two other confessions.[16] The first happens in the Lord's Prayer and is a confession that occurs before God, "Forgive us our debts as we also have forgiven our debtors" [Matthew 6:12]. Indeed the entire Lord's Prayer is a confession. For therein you confess yourself first as guilty and a sinner and beg for the grace and mercy of God. Note the individual petitions! In the Lord's Prayer you have a confession that should happen daily without ceasing. The second is the confession of the church. This should serve the following purpose: when a person has a wounded and burdened conscience, that he or she seeks comfort through God's Word.

The third is the confession that each person gives to her or his neighbor. We are all equally unrighteous. I pray "Our Father," and you do, too, in the same way. This third confession is necessary if you confess your sin to your neighbor and ask her or him to forgive you as the Lord says in Matthew 5:24, "First be reconciled with your brother or sister." We are obliged to do this, and it also stands in the Lord's Prayer, for which reason you should not complain that confession is a hard thing. In the Lord's Prayer you have this absolution: if you forgive your neighbor, then God also forgives you, and you confess here that you forgive your neighbor.

For this reason you should say: "Dear friend, I have offended you, I should not have done it." This is a true Christian confession which I owe if I have offended a brother or sister. Then that one has the duty to forgive you. If he or she does not do it, then you are absolved and have these two absolutions in the Lord's Prayer, namely, before God and before the neighbor. The third comes from God's Word, which prepares you to confess gladly. I know such from personal experience. But therefore let only those confess who would gladly be freed from their sins. We hand the others over to the pope and to his officials,[17] so that absolution and confession remain with Christians alone.

Endnotes

[1] An extensive exposition of the text, first published in Luther's Advent Postil of 1521, may be found in Lenker 1:17–58.

[2] This sermon, delivered on 29 November 1528, is also in Buchwald, 1:65–71. There Luther contrasts Jesus' kingship to the tyrants of the law, sin, and death. As only the weak accepted this lowly king in Jerusalem, so only a very poor flock in Luther's day accept the same king who comes lowlier, riding on the Word. Those who trust in and preach works are angered by the teaching of grace alone.

[3] This definition is found throughout the medieval exegetical tradition, for example in Nicholas of Lyra's commentary on the Bible, and comes from Jerome's *Liber de nominibus Hebraicis*. Modern scholarship defines the term in much the same way. See G. Kittel and G. Friedrich, eds., *Theological Dictionary of the New*

Testament, trans. by G. W. Bromiley, 10 vols. (Grand Rapids: Eerdmans, 1964–1976), 9:682–684.

[4] Called such from its first verse in Latin. This Psalm was a favorite of Luther's. See his 1530 commentary on Psalm 118 in LW 14:41–106, especially pp. 101f. on verse 25.

[5] Here Luther is depending on 16th-century Hebraists. Modern dictionaries, such as *A Hebrew and English Lexicon of the Old Testament,* ed. and trans. by F. Brown, et al. (Oxford: Clarendon Press, 1907), *loc. cit.,* translate it, "I pray" or "now" as a prayer or desire expressed.

[6] At the beginning of the sermon delivered on Sunday, March 14, 1529. See WA 29:100–118.

[7] The pastor (Luther now in his place) and three deacons.

[8] The following forms the basis of the section "A Brief Exhortation to Confession," in the Large Catechism. See BC, Large Catechism, Confession, 1–35.

[9] The obligation of all Christians for confession of sin and reception of the Sacrament of the Altar each year (usually during the Easter season) was first imposed in 1215 by the Fourth Lateran Council, convoked by Pope Innocent III. Luther attacked this practice often, for example, in his *Defense and Explanation of All the Articles* of 1521 (LW 32:61) or, more exhaustively, in *Whether the Pope Has the Authority to Make Confession Obligatory* (WA 8:129ff.).

[10] The obligation to confess all one's sins was also attacked by Luther. See, especially, *Luther's Defense and Explanation of All the Articles* (LW 32:42–44).

[11] However, in his *Discussion on How Confession Should Be Made,* of 1520 (LW 39:40f.), Luther suggests that under certain circumstances one may receive the Lord's Supper without having previously confessed.

[12] Luther expands upon this point in a section added to the Small Catechism in 1531. See BC, Small Catechism, Holy Baptism, 24–25.

[13] In 1532 Luther defended the continued use of private confession in an open letter to the town council and congregation in Frankfurt am Main (WA 30^3: 565–71). A translation of this letter by Jon D. Vieker appeared in the *Concordia Journal* 16 (1990):333–351.

[14] For the form of confession likely in use in Wittenberg at this time, see BC, Small Catechism, Baptism, 21–28, especially 28.

[15] German: *bischöflicher Gerichtsbeamter.* Luther here is referring to the diocesan judges of the late Middle Ages who heard all kinds of legal and disciplinary cases, especially regarding marriages. See BC, Small Catechism, Preface, 11.

[16] These three kinds of confession are outlined by Luther in a sermon published in 1524 (WA 15:481–505) and included in the 1525 Wittenberg edition of his "Prayer Booklet."

[17] See above, note 15.

Palm Sunday Afternoon
March 21, 1529
The Lord's Supper:
On Receiving Both Kinds

This morning we began by speaking of confession, how it must be kept and how to use it rightly according to God's Word. Now we want to talk about the Sacrament of the Body of Christ or of the Altar. Although you hear about it four times a year,[1] yet it is proper to preach on it specially, provided there is time and opportunity. For God's Word and work in the world are received in such a way that Satan does not gladly allow it to remain in its true use and essence. Therefore it is necessary to urge through teaching and admonition that we use it rightly. Because of this I have decided to speak now of the Sacrament, describing first what it is of itself and then urging that we all need this treasure, making proper use of it as long as we have it.

First, we will speak of what the Sacrament is in itself, then what attracts us to the Sacrament. Its definition is clear from the words of the Lord you have often heard. The text in the Gospels and in Paul runs like this: When Jesus sat at table in the evening and ate the Passover meal according to the law of Moses: "He took bread, gave thanks, broke it and gave it to his disciples and said, 'Take and eat. This is my body which is given for you. Do this in remembrance of me.' In the same manner after supper, he took the cup, gave thanks, gave it to them and said, 'Take and drink of it all of you. This cup is the New Testament in my blood shed for you for the forgiveness of sins. Do this, as often as you drink it, in remembrance of me.'"

These are the words which all must know. In the we are instructed what to observe and how to receive the sacrament. For Satan is as opposed to this sacrament as to the Gospel, the Word, confession, and to all other holy works. But he has practiced particular mischief on the sacrament (though also on Baptism and confession) and made a hellish torment out of it. In this text you find that Christ instituted the sacrament with his own words and calls it his body and blood. When this went into force and these words came among the people on earth, then the devil dared to change either the essence or the use and has therefore divided Christianity and wreaked indescribable havoc.

The devil is God's ape and counterfeiter of all God's work. Above all he has opposed the sacrament. Chiefly he has attempted either to remove the essence of the sacrament or to destroy its proper use. This is what I call essence: gold is gold, water is water. If someone wanted to convince me that he could make lead from gold, then he would take the essence from me and give me something so that I would think it were lead and not gold. Or if he would take the use away from me and say it is really silver or gold and would deceive me to the extent that I would throw the gold into the manure pile and would take filth for gold thinking that it were gold or would count a gold gulden for a pfennig. So the devil desired to take away the substance where he could not take away the use. He has allowed many fanatics to come teaching that the sacrament is not body and blood of Christ, but only bread and wine. This is to remove entirely the nature of the sacrament, to destroy the kernel and retain the mere husks.

When this was disputed in the world, and people held that it is truly Christ's body and blood (so that the devil had to allow the nature and essence of the sacrament to remain), he invented an abuse of it, so that a gluttonous feast was made out of it—as when the Corinthians received it with complete unworthiness, as if it were just another ordinary meal. Then the papists made a pure and simple work out of it, and those who received it did a good work and were obedient to the Christian church. Next they took one kind away and said that the other was enough.² Just when we had regained the proper usage and had reached the point where one took it by faith in God's Word and with both kinds, the devil came anew through the Enthusiasts³ and seized on the nature just as through the papists he had attacked the right use. So the sacrament is attacked from both sides.

You must learn from us so that you can judge all these fanatics and strengthen your conscience. You must know what it is and how one should use it. Allow the clear text to be your foundation and armor in order to stand not only against the fanatics of 'one kind only,' but also against the devil. Grab tightly on the key words. By them we will smite them all. And if it rained 900,000 devils daily we would still have enough in the words.⁴ There they stand, "He took the bread, he broke it, gave thanks, gave it to his disciples and said: 'This is my body.' Then he took the cup ..." The words will do it. The Enthusiasts have set themselves against these words but gain nothing.

We want to examine these Enthusiasts in order.⁵ You need no other weapon than these words! First, there are the wretched fanatics who insist so excellently on one kind, claiming that only one element must be given to the laity and whoever takes both is of the devil and damned.⁶ They say, "I stake my soul and my body on it." If they have many souls to pledge, there is one who indeed will accept them. But you may respond: I place filth on your soul and word, and set a great pile on it. If you want to go to the devil, then go ahead! But I stake everything on this, that Christ gives and institutes both kinds in the Lord's Supper and attaches to the bread and wine these words: "Do this in remembrance of me." I will stick with the bread and the cup. You stake your belly and your soul on whatever you want! Christ has died for me. But neither the pope nor you have pledged your soul for me. Christ says: "Believe in me. I will pledge my soul for you." Believe him! He is greater than you and has instituted both kinds and said: "Do this in remembrance of me."

But if they say: The Christian church has authority to change God's command, answer: Give thanks, dear Squires, that you confess that God so commanded it and Christ has so instituted this sacrament! But, they respond that the Christian church has a mandate to change God's ordinance. The second clause, in which they confess it is God's ordinance, we accept. But that the church has the authority to change such ordinances at any time it pleases, this we do not accept, but say: It is not a Christian church that changes God's ordinance, rather it is the devil. For God has not ordered his affairs in such a way that he commands humans to change them. If the church had this authority, where would we stand? If I concede that the church has authority to change one part, then I open up all the doors and windows to the devil to change everything that God has commanded. Then the church could also order that one need not believe in Christ and could abolish the Ten Commandments.

But therefore the church is commended in the Scripture, as is written in Ephesians 5:23, that it is subject to Christ like a wife to her husband. Now an upright man indeed permits and tolerates the woman to be master over the domestic help and the children. But if the husband has ordered something in the house, and she wants to break it, that he would not tolerate. In the same way the Christian church is subject to Christ and what Christ has ordered; to this it holds, and it hearkens to him. They even admit this themselves, but say and do the opposite. Thus they lie like scoundrels. That they confess it is God's ordinance is true, but the other part is false.

Indeed they have adduced many examples, but they are laughable and prove nothing—for example, when God says to Jeremiah, "See, today I appoint you over nations and over kingdoms, to pluck up and to pull down, to destroy and to overthrow, to build and to plant" (Jeremiah 1:10). The jackass Cochlaeus has trotted out this text.[7] Therefore they conclude: If the holy prophet had the authority to destroy and to plant, should not the church have the authority to destroy and to plant? The text says that Jeremiah is placed over nations and kingdoms, that with God's Word he is to punish and proclaim the destruction of kingdoms. But the text does not say: I have placed you over God and his Word and work, that you should destroy it. One should crown such asses with donkey farts.[8] Who has ever heard of such an interpretation? "Nations" and "kingdoms" mean God's Word? That would be like commanding my servant or maid that they should have the authority to milk the cows whenever they want. Then a son would also be over his father! I say this so that you see how foolish those are who today fight against the Gospel. I am in the place of the prophet Jeremiah; I am with you in Wittenberg to plant and to build up. Therefore I will conclude: I have authority over God and his Word.

Further they object: The church has accepted the four gospels, others they have not accepted. Thus the church is master over them. If not, who would know which gospel were true,[9] perhaps Bartholomew's gospel[10] or another? That sounds just as if we had the gospels from the church and not from God. Christianity has accepted the book, they say, therefore Christianity is over the book. I accept the teaching of Paul, therefore I am over his teaching. Oh, that they had made the distinction between confessing and having authority! The Christian church confesses that the teaching, the Gospel, the book are true. But thereby the church is not given the authority over it. Then I could also say: I accept Christ, therefore I am over Christ. Or I would say of the prince of the land: Duke Hans of Saxony is my prince, not Duke George and the Margrave.[11] I accept the former, not the latter; therefore because he is my prince, I am over him. Would he allow this? Would he allow his command to be changed? Is that indeed consistent?

Similarly, a lawyer could say: This command the emperor has fixed, that one a false teacher has fixed. Therefore this scholar stands over the emperor because he can distinguish between what the emperor has fixed and what another fixes. You've got to be kidding yourself! So they conclude quite foolishly: The Christian church confesses that this book and its teaching are true, therefore it is over them. These are rotten hoaxes. Christ has given the church this authority, to separate between truth and falsehood, as he says in Matthew 7:15: "Beware of false prophets!" When the evangelical teaching spread throughout the world from the apostles, upright teachers saw and received it; but other books that did not correspond to this, they discarded. So we also do. But I cannot conclude: Because I accept John's gospel, I am over the same. For this reason say: It is not true; the Christian church does not have the authority to change a single letter. For it is written in Matthew 5:19, "Whoever breaks one of the least of these commandments, and teaches others to do the same, will be called least in the kingdom of heaven." Add nothing and take nothing away. It should remain as Christ has ordered it.

But here God's ordinance concerns the two kinds of the sacrament, bread and wine, body and blood. Whoever changes this is not of the Christian church, but of the synagogue of the devil. The Christian church has no authority to change anything but only to judge, so that we do not accept false teaching as true. The Gospel was not written first, but first the apostles had to preach it orally. Therefore it cannot be said that the church is over the Gospel. Only confession, judgment, recognition of what is false and true, is within the Christian church's authority. Therefore I can indeed recognize whether your wife is upright, but still I have no authority over her. For this reason they are crude buffoons who conclude: I can recognize this and judge it; therefore I am over it. But their desire to have the power to change amounts to nothing. The Christian church has accepted only the Gospel, and the Gospel has stood by the church. Whether St. Bartholomew's gospel is right or not, the church has accepted the true Gospel. The church has had the true Gospel from the beginning and from this has judged what is unjust and false.

Their behavior corresponds to the saying: "Tatters surround a lie. If one wants to embellish a lie, one must sew together seven patched up lies." That is, if someone intends to justify a lie, he must have seven others; but when those seven come, he must once again have seven times as many. Therefore everything of theirs is a lie. Now whatever they want to say, you respond: *Verbum Dei manet in aeternum*! "God's Word endures forever!"[12] So you confess that it is God's Word—good! But that the church should have the power to change it, to this we say: No! But because we have the correct understanding, we enjoy the Sacrament under both kinds. These are the greatest arguments of the papists. But first and foremost the text states: "He took the bread, gave thanks and gave it to them. Afterwards he took the cup, etc." That is Christ's Word and ordinance. For this reason both kinds belong to the whole of Christianity. All who proceed to change it, even if they stake soul or body on it, act like scoundrels.

But further, they come to the word "disciples" and say he has given the Sacrament only to his disciples. I never heard of this. Read the Acts of the Apostles! There you will find that disciples are not only the apostles, but all who would believe in Christ. Therefore it is written, "Now in Joppa there was a disciple whose name was Tabitha" (Acts 9:36). In the word "disciple" we are all included. The uneducated heads must blush, that even a woman is expressly called a disciple. And without a doubt women were also at the Last Supper, like Mary Magdalene, Martha and Johanna, and freely ate with him, after they cooked the Passover meal and paschal lamb. It does not say that he gave it to the apostles or the priests but to his disciples. Stand on this! The evangelists speak very differently of the disciples and the apostles. Disciples are also those who cling to Christ, not only the apostles. At Antioch they began to call the disciples *Christians* (Acts 11:26), but not at Jerusalem. There they are called pupils *disciples of Jesus Christ,* and so it is to this very day. But as the name of Christian and disciple is intended for all people—men and women—so the text also applies to all of us.

Because their argument does not hold water, they even abandon the text and say, "Christ has made priests here." But if that is true, then the laity have no element at all, for Christ says both things to his disciples: eat and drink! Therefore they defile themselves in their wisdom. Yes, this is true, they say, both kinds are given to the priests. But the church has ordered this and is not God's ordinance. A plague on your house![13] God forgive me for they say: According to the Gospel, neither one nor two kinds belong to the laity. That they have even one comes from the concession of the church! But for over a thousand years the church gave the laity both kinds. Now, if the Christian church so long understood it in no other way, then we do Christianity an injustice by offering only one kind to the laity.

From the words of the text you should therefore conclude: Christ gave his disciples bread and wine. Now ask: What is a *disciple*? If they say an apostle or a priest, let them prove it. No, everyone—man or woman—who has accepted Christ's teaching is Christ's disciple. For the Greek word *disciple* means *pupil*; disciples are those who are trained, taught and who let themselves be taught.

In conclusion: The Sacrament is bread and wine, that is, the body and blood of Christ; both are to be offered to every Christian. But Satan does not tolerate this, for this reason he desecrates it. Concerning the other abuses we will speak tomorrow.

Endnotes

[1]Preachers in Wittenberg held weekday sermons on the catechism four times during the year, in March, May, September, and December. In the absence of Johannes Bugenhagen (1485-1558) during 1528, Luther preached on the catechism three times. These sermons became the basis for both the Large and Small Catechisms, which Luther began to write in December 1528. For the third set of catechetical sermons, see LW 51:133–93.

[2]According to the scholastic theologians, such as Thomas Aquinas (1225/6–1274) and William of Occam (ca. 1285–1349), the mass was effective *ex opere operato,* that is, on the basis of the performance of the rite. The performance of this rite or the payment for its performance was a good work. In 1215 at the Lateran IV Council the practice of withholding the cup from the laity was approved. Luther

attacked both notions in many places, notably in *The Babylonian Captivity of the Church* (LW 36:19–57).

[3]German: *Schwärmer*. Luther also uses the word "fanatics" or "sacramentarians" to describe those who reject the real presence of Christ in the Lord's Supper. He employed this derisive term, which designated those around whose heads wild ravings or dreams swarmed like bees or flies, first for Andrew Karlstadt (ca. 1480–1541), a former teacher in Wittenberg, and then Ulrich Zwingli (1484–1531), the head preacher in Zurich, and his followers. See, for example, *The Sacrament of the Body and Blood of Christ—Against the Fanatics* (LW 36:327–61). They rejected the clear testimony of Scripture in favor of their own internal dreams and reason.

[4]See Luther in his letter of 5 March 1522 to the Elector Frederick (LW 48:391): "And if it rained nothing but Duke Georges for nine days." The third verse of "A Mighty Fortress" (LW 53:285) shows this same kind of defiance.

[5]Here and elsewhere Luther equates his Roman and Swiss opponents, calling them all *Schwärmer*, because in his eyes they all opposed the clear word of Scripture with their own reason and authority.

[6]Two kinds were first received by the people during Luther's absence in the Wartburg in 1521. Upon his return he objected to the way the change was made (LW 51:90f.), and in the *Instructions for the Visitors of Parish Pastors in Electoral Saxony* of 1528, while insisting only communion in both kinds be preached, he still allowed the weak to commune using one kind (LW 40:289–92).

[7]John Cochlaeus (1479–1552) was one of Luther's most formidable opponents. He was an advisor to Duke George of Saxony and attacked Luther throughout his career, beginning already at the Diet of Worms in 1521. In 1529 he mocked Luther and the Saxon visitation in a tract entitled *Martinus Lutherus Septiceps* (The Seven-Headed Martin Luther) with a title page depicting Luther with seven heads. See Heiko Oberman, *Luther: Man between God and the Devil*, trans. by E. Walliser-Schwarzbart (New Haven: Yale University Press, 1989), 4.

[8]A kind of thistle hunted after by the donkey.

[9]Nearly all reformers, including Luther, had to explain the famous dictum of Augustine (354–430), bishop of Hippo, "But I would not have believed the gospel, unless the authority of the catholic church had moved me" (in *Against the Epistle of Manichaeus*, vi). Luther addresses this text in *A Reply to the Texts Cited in Defense of the Doctrines of Men* of 1522 (LW 35:150–53). A translation of Augustine's work is found in NPNF, series 1, 4:131.

[10]An apocryphal gospel referred to by Jerome and Bede. See *The Oxford Dictionary of the Christian Church*, 2nd ed. F. L. Cross, et al. (Oxford: Oxford University Press, 1964), loc. cit.

[11]Luther is referring to John [Hans], Elector of Saxony (1468-1532), George, Duke of Saxony (1471–1539), Luther's implacable enemy, and Joachim I, Margrave and Elector of Brandenburg (1484–1535).

[12]The Latin abbreviation, *VDMA* (cf. Isaiah 40:8 and 1 Peter 1:24–25), was first used as a motto for the Saxon elector in 1522. For details, see F. J. Stopp, "Verbum Domini Manet in Aeternum, the Dissemination of a Reformation Slogan, 1522–1904," *Lutheran Quarterly*, n.s., 1 (1987): 54–71.

[13]Literal translation: "May you shake with fever!"

Monday Morning, Holy Week
March 22, 1529
The Lord's Supper
On the Real Presence

Yesterday we heard about one part of the Sacrament, namely, that you should know what it is and how one should use and enjoy it. Further we want to urge you to consider it precious, dear, and valuable.

Since times are now so dangerous and Satan so foolish that he lays hold of our sacraments, all Christians should study until they are so certain of this material that they may defend themselves when the fanatics come. The evangelists are in precise agreement with one another. In these words lie our refuge, treasure, and comfort, not only to feed us but also to defend us.

First of all, the papists have taken away half of this Sacrament and would persuade us with a flood of words that we receive just as much in the bread alone as in both kinds. Pay no attention to them for here stand the words that Christ himself has ordered. Let neither the devil nor an angel drive you from them. Let them prattle on as long as they want. But those who struggle in the front lines and are evangelists should read the words more carefully. Then they will find that our reasons are absolutely firm but those of our adversaries, on the other hand, collapse. They should set nothing over conscience and God's Word.

But then the devil comes with annoying fanatics who take the Sacrament away totally, where the papists only took half. At least the pope left half of the Sacrament and confessed it as a Sacrament. The Enthusiasts, who now rattle around in the Sacrament, attack it in league with the devil and fill a great part of the world with their fanaticism. The papists and the scholastics still clung to the true body and blood of Christ, but the fanatics deny it and destroy the entire Sacrament. Against this you must defend yourself with the clear and plain words: "He took bread, gave thanks, broke it and gave it to them, saying, Take and eat." These are straightforward and clear words: He had the bread in his hands.[1] Therefore you can understand what he is talking about when he says, "Take and eat." He must be speaking about the bread, and he specially repeats himself by saying, "Take and eat!" Taking bread in your hands is not a dream or an illusion but a true work. And he broke it, that is, he himself gave it and commanded them: "Eat."

And while he commands us to eat and drink, he says: "This is my body," "This is my blood." No language on earth can express anything other than that this bread is Christ's body. So that there can be no excuse for misinterpretation, he adds that it is the body which is "given for us" and the blood which is "shed for you for the forgiveness of sins." We certainly have no other body that accomplishes this than the body of Christ. Because of this they cannot deny that it is Christ's body in the Lord's Supper. They insist that it is figurative speech! However, as I have already said, one should not change God's words—not even a letter. In the entire Scripture, it is unheard of that "it is" should mean "it signifies."[2] For this reason stick with the words. Then you will be sure that Christ took the bread, broke and gave it, and spoke over it: It is his body. Stick with the words; he will not deceive you.

Here we must separate our reason from God's Word. You must put out the eyes of reason and toss them into the pit of hell. Instead you must let God's Word be true and cling to it with closed eyes and ears. This is the flaw of the fanatical spirits in this matter, that they let their reason advise whether it is possible that bread and wine can be body and blood. Reason cannot understand this and then adorns itself with a peacock feather and accepts instead this article, "Jesus ascended into heaven," and says: If he ascended, he cannot be in the bread. For these are opposites: that he is in heaven and that he is held in the hand of a scoundrel on earth. With this reason at once concludes, the bread and wine are not Christ's body and blood since he is in heaven. There they stand: they promote this and blow this with all their bellows.

But you may answer: I believe the same as you do, that Christ ascended into heaven. However, that on this account those words should be false, this I still don't believe. This argument is never proved: Christ ascended into heaven and sits at the right hand of God, therefore his body cannot be in the bread. For we indeed have stories in the New Testament that Christ, after he ascended into heaven, was still here below. He appeared to Peter and the others beside the Sea of Galilee, to Paul on the road to Damascus and another time in the temple in Jerusalem.[3] If this is true, why should he not also be able to appear in our places? For this reason, speak in this way: My reason is foolish and deceives, but Christ's word does not deceive. Therefore I stick with the words: This is Christ's body! But how it happens and how it is possible, that I do not know. Do not admit the whore reason[4] with this question! Otherwise, it's all over.

For example, the devil tripped our first parents Adam and Eve with the reasonable question: What might be God's motive for commanding you to eat of all the trees of the garden except this one? As if the devil wanted to say: God is not so foolish that he should have forbidden this. Reason immediately supposed: Does it even make sense that God forbids a single tree and permits an entire forest? And so they firmly concluded: God has not commanded it.

It is the same way here: Christ ascended into heaven. Therefore, why do you construct this article of faith, that he is in the bread? Reason at once says: This argument is clearly true; therefore it is not Christ's body. But Christians should put reason under lock and key, or they will hold to no article of faith. If you measure the articles of faith by the capabilities of reason, then you are still more blind than Arius and Cerinthus.[5] For there are still greater articles than this one. We fall into a trap like the Arians and the Turks.[6] They thought: How can this be that three divine persons are one God? Ask reason for advice and you are immediately trapped. The Turks and the Jews mock us exceedingly about this Sacrament. And when the Turks hear that Christians eat their God they say, A more foolish thing has never been uttered! If the door is opened for the devil to ask, Why has God said this? How does one make sense of it? then he certainly wins. If the snake sticks in its head, the entire body immediately follows.

Here there are no obscure words, but words that are crystal clear: He took the bread, gave thanks, broke it and gave it to them, saying, "Take and eat. This is my body." This is an amazingly clear word. He does not say: Some sort of feed, but bread, as the children call it, which the mother or the father breaks. Moreover, he gave simple instructions, "Take and eat." This is not obscure. Indeed, if he had used obscure words, as in Psalm 3:7 ("You break the teeth of the wicked"), then one might think: What are the teeth? Is the mouth meant? Or in the Gospel, "Beware of the yeast of the Pharisees and the yeast of Herod" (Mark 8:15). Or Luke 8:11: "The seed is the Word of God." But here are such clear words that cannot allow a metaphorical interpretation, since they speak of a bodily taking, administering and eating so that one cannot ignore them without doing violence to the words.[7] If they want to mangle the language, watch this! I, too, could say: mother means whore, father means fornicator. Then no one could speak with another any more. Let those who want to remain with the truth see to it that they hold to the words given in the sacraments. If you stick with the words, you will be certain. But if you let in Satan with his questions, it will be all over with you.

This applies to learned people who reject Satan. I advise the uneducated not to get that involved in this dispute. If God allowed it, you would soon go astray, for Satan can also whet and sharpen his tongue, so that the people fall away from the words; after that it's all over for them. I know the toil and sweat that it requires to continue to stick to the simple words. If Satan finds me idle and without God's Word, then he shoots with a poisonous arrow. He is a master of this and lies in wait for this: If he finds the heart burdened and busied with other thoughts, then he is there and causes people to go astray, so that they get completely lost. The fanatical spirits know nothing about such things. But I know a great part of Satan's craft.[8] He seeks either to find an idle house without Scripture or to take away the Word. In this way he tempted Adam. God's command was stuck in Adam's heart, but Satan said: It is true, it is indeed God's command, but why? As soon as the commandment left their hearts, they died. However, Satan does not remain with you if he sees that you firmly grasp the Word with both hands; then he does not come because he fears the cutting edge of the Word, and he leaves you truly in peace.

It is complete rubbish that certainty does not know his trickery.[9] For this reason I admonish you to stick with the words. If you hold fast to them and a fanatical spirit comes, do not listen to such a person but pay attention instead to the words. Therefore if fanatical spirits come to me with their reasons, they are the same to me as a fool. But if I abandon the Word, I would be lost. But they say: How do I make sense of this? Christ is sitting in heaven above and is in the bread? The devil has so fixed this in their hearts that they cannot hear. When I hear their words they go in one ear and out the other. It is not even necessary to answer them. I do not accept their silly words. I would also not want to do them the honor of refuting all their words, as they do mine with the greatest effort. When one builds a house, it requires effort, and then the wind comes [Matthew 7:24–28], that is, be certain that you will have no rest and peace!

For this reason take care to ground your conscience in the Word! Then we would indeed escape the storm. But if you build on sand, you will not escape. There are those who completely rip the Sacrament to shreds so that nothing remains. With the papists at least the one kind remained. But with us who have the Word, the Sacrament remains the true body and the true blood of Christ. How that happens, you are not to know. Faith and sight are different from one another. What one believes, one does not see, and what one sees, one does not believe. How a mother remains a virgin, that I cannot grasp. The Jews laugh about this and about the fact that the Son of God allows himself to die so shamefully and that God and man are one person. Bread is bread and wine is wine to the Turks, pagans and cows. For this reason it is no great art if this is taught. If something is perceptible, then it is not an article of faith. We believe that Christ has given us his body and his blood in this Sacrament, as his words say.

First and foremost, one must therefore learn to stick purely and precisely with the Word. If people want to fight against their enemies, let them do it as those who are ready for it and are skilled! Not all are skillful at this or as learned as they might be. Satan can indeed topple such learning. Teach one another the words and stick with them and say: The words are so clear, like a mother and child speak, spoken most simply. They are without any obscurity; as they stand may they remain! Whenever Jesus Christ tempts, no harm is done. Therefore these words "conceived of the Holy Spirit, born of the virgin Mary," are clear. "Born" means "born" and "virgin'"means "virgin." If the words are so clear, you need no explanation. I do not say such a thing without good reason. It is the devil who wants to make the obscure words clear and the clear words obscure. This is his art.

Now we will speak of the true essence of the Sacrament. What is its essence? What belongs to the Sacrament of the Altar? The Sacrament consists of three parts: God's command, the elements of bread and wine, and the promise. God's Word belongs to the Sacrament, indeed this above all; after that belongs what one touches and perceives. But that Word is twofold: command and promise. As it is in Baptism: God commands, "Go into all the world and baptize!" [Matthew 28:19] and he promises, "whoever believes and is baptized will be saved" [Mark 16:16]. In the Sacrament of the Altar there is the material part, bread and wine, and in them the body and blood of Christ. Secondly, there is his vow by which he binds himself to us and something is pledged: This is my body, given for you. When God makes a covenant with us, he promises something to us; we receive it and promise to keep it. These are the true vows of God in Scripture and in the psalms.

"This is my body, given for you." These words do not command us to do something but sound as if someone were promising and bestowing something on me, because he says, "Take it," not "Do something!" Here nothing is commanded, it is only bestowed, promised and given. Whoever embraces this covenant receives the promise. Therefore bread and wine is one part of the Sacrament. Then the Word bears his vow and promise. Therefore, what belongs to a sacrament is, first of all, that there is something like bread and wine; secondly, that there is the word of his vow and promise. These two make the sacrament: a material thing like bread and wine and the word which reads: "This is my body, given for you." The third is that God orders, institutes and commands: "Do this in remembrance of me." There he does not give, but demands. First he gives and binds himself to that which he will do; but the second thing we must do: "Do this in remembrance of me." If you rightly learn these words, then you will rightly understand the Sacrament: First a material thing, second a word; these two make the Sacrament.

Because of this you will be able to answer easily the abuse of the Sacrament that has covered the earth. Some people are troubled whether an evil priest could rightly perform the Sacrament, whether he can baptize or administer the Sacrament when he himself does not believe. This created a great stir and still does.[10] Therefore they say: How could he, who is not himself clean, be able to make another clean? If a servant has unclean hands, how can he make a glass clean? What is itself unclean cannot make clean. They then conclude: An evil priest cannot baptize or administer the Sacrament. This error is checked with these words: "Take and eat." There it stands that the Sacrament does not depend on the priest's holiness or righteousness but on Christ's words alone.

The priest makes neither the Sacrament of the Altar nor Baptism—though he allows it to occur—indeed not even Peter or Paul or an angel can. But the Sacrament depends on the Word. The material thing is bread and wine; the Word is "This is my body," "This is my blood." But who says this? These are not the priest's words—no more than the words, "I baptize" are. They are the words of him who took the bread in his hand and said, "Take and eat." He did not take the bread, give it and say: This is what you should say! but he said so himself. However, when the priest takes it in his hand and distributes it, we say whether the priest believes or not, if he administers the Sacrament, then he gives us Christ's body and blood.

God can also speak through a donkey [Numbers 22:21–41]. To be sure, no one should take offense at this error. Even famous people have become involved in this. Cyprian rebaptized heretics who had previously been baptized. Pay attention then! The Sacrament is based not on human holiness but on God's Word! Otherwise I could never receive the Sacrament, listen to a sermon, or undergo Baptism.

The devil is able to pervert it at once by asking: How can I know whether someone is righteous? They say, "You will know them by their fruits" [Matthew 7:20]. Indeed! Then we would have nothing at all from the Gospel and the Sacraments. A righteous person could go to the altar righteous and become evil while standing at the altar. Human righteousness trembles like an aspen leaf. But I will not set my faith on such a leaf. These people are so foolish as when one would say: If a righteous person preaches the Gospel, then I will believe the Word; if a godless person preaches, I will not believe. But God has established the Sacrament on himself, on his Word, and on his promise. This is the true body and the true blood of Christ not because the priest is holy, but because you hear the Word, the promise, and vow, that he adds to it by saying: "This is my body," "This is my blood."

This is the one abuse whereby the devil attacks the Sacrament. But suppose you say: the Sacrament is bread and wine and the Word in addition! That's it! If this Word did not stand there it would be only bread and wine, such as you eat at the table. But because these words have been added to it, it is something else. These words are not a matter of human righteousness but of God's Word. It is the same with Baptism. These are not words of Peter or Judas and yet each of them can speak them. Though Peter or the devil say it, they are God's words. I would have no regard for St. Peter if Christ had not previously said, "Go and baptize!" In the same way I would also have no regard for the bread even if a hundred psalms were spoken over it. The sanctity of the psalms do not make the body of Christ, so instead I run to the Word of Christ, whether a scoundrel gives me the Sacrament or someone else.

Ignore those who say: See what an excellent office a priest has! He can bring Christ down from heaven.[11] They talked us poor people into this. For this reason you say a priest is superior to every angel or our own dear lady Mary. Shame on you! It is not a person's word and work, but God's. Therefore do not look at your work! The priest does nothing but move his hand and mouth. The word and work remain God's.

The fanatical spirits make themselves useless beyond all measure with the matter. Therefore they revile us: You new papists want to save the people with bread and wine, with a handful of bread! Do you think that by your hissing God is going to come down from heaven and creep into in the bread? When the common folk hear such things, they let themselves be deceived with sharp arguments. But let my backside be shown to you, O Satan![12]

We have never taught that only bread and wine are in the Sacrament. Instead we have said there are two parts to the Sacrament, namely, bread and wine and God's Word. But they do not have the Sacrament at all; for without the Word it is no sacrament. But how does it seem to you when Jesus comes here and says, "This is my body," "This is my blood"? Is it then merely bread and wine? This is what they want to hide from the eyes of the people. The pope did the same thing.

All who attack the Sacrament attempt to obscure the words, as the pope has done. When someone twists the words and makes "it signifies" out of "it is," it's all over for the Sacrament. But you may respond to such a person: You crude jackass, do not mutilate the Sacrament for me! You take the Word from me which is the kernel and leave me with the husks; that is, with bread and wine. Christ said, "This is my body"—that is the kernel! The words make the Sacrament, just as grain has a husk and a kernel. The water in Baptism is a husk, but when the Word is added, along comes the kernel and it is no longer only a husk. When you let the Sacrament be divided for you and take away the kernel, then it is all over.

A sacrament is a created element with God's Word in it.[13] You must ascribe more to the Word than to the created element; indeed everything to the Word, nothing to the created element, because the created element's appearance is only a husk where the Word is lacking. All errors come from removing the Word. If you keep the Word, you stand up to the pope and the fanatics and those who think a priest is superior to the laity. The problem is that one regards the Sacrament as a mere created element or as a human work. The pope says the priest offers a sacrifice in the Sacrament. All this arises from the fact that one regards it as a human work. But we regard it as God's work adorned with God's Word.

Tomorrow we will recount the pope's error so that you learn to recognize this Sacrament well and clearly.

Endnotes

[1] Andreas Karlstadt, at one time Luther's colleague at the University of Wittenberg, argued that when Jesus said, "This is my body," he was pointing to his

own body. Thus the word "this" referred not to the bread but to the physical body of Jesus.

[2] Here Luther refers to the chief disagreement between himself and Ulrich Zwingli. See, for example, *That These Words of Christ, 'This Is My Body,' Etc., Still Stand Firm against the Fanatics*, a tract from 1527 (LW 37:3–150).

[3] John 21, Acts 9, and Acts 7. Luther indicates that the resurrection appearance in John 21 occurred after the Ascension.

[4] Luther's customary way of describing the seductive power of reason.

[5] Arians were named after Arius (ca. 250–ca. 336), a priest of Alexandria, Egypt, who taught that Christ was not fully God but that "there was [a time] when he was not." Cerinthus (ca. 100) was a gnostic who held that Jesus was less than God.

[6] Luther sometimes used the term Turks, as here, to denote the followers of Islam. Like the Arians, they rejected the Trinity.

[7] Ulrich Zwingli argued that the phrase "This is my body" was a trope and had to be interpreted metaphorically.

[8] Luther often spoke of Satan's attacks (*Anfechtungen*) against him. One of his greatest spiritual crises came in the second half of 1527. See Heiko A. Oberman, *Luther: Man between God and the Devil* (New Haven: Yale University Press, 1989), 320–324.

[9] Medieval theologians often warned against *securitas* (security) as giving leave to the devil. This was contrasted to the godly virtue of fear. Thus, according to Luther's account of their meeting in Augsburg in 1518, Cardinal Cajetan (1469–1534) attacked Luther's explanation to the seventh of the 95 Theses on the grounds that Luther's demand for faith in the priest's absolution contradicted the uncertainty one should have about whether grace would be received. See LW 31:261, 270–275.

[10] This issue was first raised by the Donatists in North Africa, who broke with the Catholic church over the presence among the bishops of certain "traitors" who had handed over the church's sacred books during the Diocletian persecution of A.D. 303. Augustine opposed them in various tracts and sermons. Their position was revived by certain Anabaptists, who argued that if the pope was the Antichrist sacraments performed under the pope, especially Holy Baptism, were invalid. See BC, Augsburg Confession, VIII, and Luther's *Concerning Rebaptism*, LW 40: 230–234.

[11] Luther here refers to certain aspects of late-medieval piety, which imagined that by virtue of his ordination the priest possessed the grace to bring Christ into the sacrament.

[12] For the scatological nature of Luther's comments about the devil, see Heiko Oberman, *Luther: Man between God and the Devil* (New Haven: Yale University Press, 1989), 106–109.

[13] Here and elsewhere in this sermon Luther is paraphrasing Augustine's statement from his sermon on John 15:3, "The word is added to the element, and it becomes a sacrament." See his *Homilies on the Gospel of John* in NPNF, series 1, 7:344.

Tuesday Morning, Holy Week
March 23, 1529
The Lord's Supper
On Not Making the Sacrament a Work

We have already indicated some abuses and errors regarding this Sacrament. Now we propose to take up in more detail the errors that the pope has directed against us. It is very important not to forget these errors. For as we begin to forget them, we also forget about the words of God and the Sacrament itself. Where the Word is lacking, there is no stability. But now it is their total aim to take the Word from us or twist it. We have written a lot about it, we sing it, we have preached it and painted it on paper.[1] However, they still do not read the words connected with the Sacrament. Instead, with them only custom and what the ancient Fathers have written is true. But in order to understand the words and the Sacrament better, we must consider these errors carefully.

You have heard the error that the priests have made themselves greater lords than the angels and the mother Mary and have made a work of the Sacrament.[2] They did not realize that the Sacrament is a promise and a covenant in which Christ's body and blood are given to us. You older folk know this, you who were with us under the papacy. At that time no one thought to seek help, comfort, salvation here, but instead one came to perform a work in the Sacrament, just as the people in the papacy are driven to do this down to this day.

This is a noteworthy, great and terrible abuse that has filled the entire world: they perform the Sacrament as a good work and only care about the command of the church. Anyone could overturn this error and abuse by simply looking at the phrase "and gave it to them." Certainly it is a gift as the text says. And he himself says: "Take." Therefore it is sheer gift. Why do they not look at the words? Because Satan will have it so, that the people do not rightly recognize the Sacrament but remain with their old trumpery. For this reason if you simply grasp the Word rightly, you could crush the abuse that is in the entire world. The text reads "given"; we have not compelled Christ in the Sacrament, but he bequeathed it voluntarily. It says given, taken, eaten, drunk, praised, thanked—not wrung out by force. But they will not look at this, but close their eyes and consider the Sacrament as a work of obedience. I fear this atrocity is so great that it will be punished not with a temporal but an eternal punishment. Further, there are still more abuses in addition to the fact that the laity forgets the words of faith and does not want to receive the Sacrament as a gift for their souls.

The priests are much more wicked and have gone into the corner, have read the mass, and have not received it as a gift, but as a sacrifice. Then these wretched people have given it to themselves; of their own authority they took it and sold it to others.[3] This abuse has also arisen from the fact that the Word was taken away. But now that abuse has been set aside.

Look at what miserable abuse that was. The Sacrament is not given to individuals for themselves alone, so that the priest may go and eat for himself. The text says there should be at least two or three.[4] For this reason the Fathers also called it *Synaxis*, communion, a distribution in a group. But the priest does the opposite, considers it as a work, and uses it only for himself. He does not look at the words: "This is my body, given for you." "Given for you," refers to the group. If he would consider the words he would be horrified, leave his mass, and throw away chasuble and stole. The Sacrament is a great gift given for many, and he sacrifices it for himself alone. The words "given for you" set aside all private masses, but they don't want to see it. Does the "for you" perhaps mean "for a god in heaven"? We have turned it around, and made the mass into a sacrifice that we do. "We sacrifice to you," they have said. But the Sacrament is given to us as a gift, and they throw it up into heaven. This is what happens when one allows the Word to fall away. But the words say with certainty: It is a gift given to us—to me, to you and to all. With these words you can overthrow everything that the pope has introduced.

Now look what has resulted from making a work of the Sacrament! Everyone sold the Sacrament, and from this masses, altars, monasteries, and yearly processions have been founded: I give so many hundred gulden to this altar for me and all my relations so that we all benefit from the divine office. In taking such gifts they claimed to make satisfaction before God for the people. What did they do wrong? They did not look at the words, which read: "This is my body, given for you." These words do not allow themselves to be sold, but whoever believes them has their fruit and vice versa.

This very buying and selling is so widespread that the mass ruled the world. Simply look at the masses at the annual fair: for the journey, for good fortune, for love-making. They have thrown everything in the cup. The miser and every one else has placed their money in the mass. Are these not terrible abuses? No one thought about this because no one was concerned about the words. Instead they became stuck in the notion that the Sacrament is the body and blood of Christ, offered for the sins of the dead and the living. The pope zealously forbade the priests from saying the words of institution to the laity. So the words fell into oblivion for us and also for themselves, so that they remained completely unaware of the words, and instead clung to the mere work.

But the most terrible abuse is the last: every priest has made himself a mediator of Christ. All this arises from the fact that they have not looked at the words. Even in the words and Sacrament, where Christ is called a mediator, he, the "priestlet,"[5] intervenes and calls himself a mediator. Just look at the text of the mass, and you will certainly find it that it is so. What is God's work alone, they have claimed for themselves with their masses.

Thomas differentiated between the *opus operatum* and the *opus operantis*.[6] The mass is a work, but with this distinction. At one and the same time, it is an *opus operantis*, the work that the priest does, and the *opus operatum*, the body of Christ in the Sacrament. Because the *opus operatum* (the Sacrament) is present, therefore, they say, the mass (the *opus operantis*) is so great. If it were just the priests' work, it would not be so great. But because of the *opus operatum* he can sell it and help others. Is this not an immeasurably terrible thing? These people, who should communicate the words of Christ and the Sacrament according to Christ's institution, sacrifice it to God as if they themselves were mediators, when in fact Christ is the sole mediator. Here the priest wants to be a mediator and make Christ into the sacrifice. Therefore the Sacrament was sold for such a high price, because it is in itself so great a thing that heaven and earth cannot pay for it.

But Christ has instituted the Sacrament for us to take, use, and enjoy, and he has done this in order to exercise his mediatorial office over us in that he says: "This is my body, given for you." And therefore the Sacrament is nothing other than an exercise of his mediatorial office. But then the "priestlet"[7] intervenes and wants to make Christ into a sacrifice and to reconcile us with the Father and with Christ, as if Christ did not have the strength to do it himself. The atrocity is so great that I am at a loss for words.

But we should put aside such abuses. That happens when we look at the words carefully. They have made the Sacrament a sacrifice to God, when it is nothing other than a gift, namely, the body and blood of Christ given to us to eat, to drink, and to receive. I am surprised that the papists do not look at their own big traps. For there is the work: that they must eat and drink and say the words of Christ that call it a gift. Nevertheless they act against their own words and Christ's, which they see before their very eyes. If eating and drinking in the Sacrament is a sacrifice, then everything that Christ gives to me is called a work and a sacrifice that I give to God. They eat it, enjoy it and receive it, and yet they call it a work and a sacrifice, not a gift.

My eyes and ears are a gift of God. But if I would follow these foolish people, then I would have to say: By the fact that I see and hear, I offer a sacrifice to God. In the same way you would have to call your children, house and farm, fields, money, and everything that you have not a gift of God, but a sacrifice. Although they recognize it with their own words and confess that they receive something when they eat and drink the body and blood of Christ, yet they persist in their godlessness and refuse to budge from their abuse, but say: " I have resolved that I will give it to God as a work and a sacrifice and not receive it from him as a gift, despite the fact that I call it a sacrament."

Now Christians should give thanks for all gifts. This is the sacrifice, as in Psalm 50:14: "Offer to God a sacrifice of thanksgiving, and pay your vows to the Most High." And Christ says, "Do this in remembrance of me!"[8] What is given to us, which comes from Christ for our good, is reasonably called a gift that we should enjoy, not give and sacrifice to God. For this reason I have most diligently urged you to learn what the Sacrament is. We say: A Sacrament is bread and wine in and with the words, "Take and eat. This is my body." You should regard these words as precious, and you should judge everything according to them and cling to them. Indeed they state that in the Sacrament the body and blood of Christ are present. They teach with certainty that it is not mere bread and wine.

You can overturn every error of both the papists and the Enthusiasts when you stick precisely and purely with the words. If the words are snatched away, then you cannot curb error. I think this is said bluntly enough. The Sacrament is made perfectly clear when you say: It is bread and wine comprehended in these words, "He took bread ...." These words can preserve you in a pure understanding of this Sacrament and its Christian use, so that we possess the Sacrament in all its purity.

But our adversaries have one thing against us: We do not call the Sacrament a sacrifice, but, they say, Augustine and Ambrose call it a sacrifice![9] What shall we say to this? So they have such a word from the Fathers; that alone must be the sun to them! I answer in this way: the Father and Christ speak thus; what Augustine said counts for nothing. We want to hear what Christ says. But, they object, we should look to what Augustine and Ambrose say! To this we answer: We honor each one of the Fathers in his gifts that are given him, but we do not place them over Christ. If I must reject one, Christ or Augustine, then I would rather reject Augustine. There stand the plain words of Christ. That some call it a sacrifice, I let pass. They have not given one reason for their characterization. For this reason Augustine and Ambrose hardly move me to call it a sacrifice contrary to the words of Christ. I have still not heard that one must believe Augustine over Christ. No one is duty bound to believe me. But one must obey Christ.

Now to any and all of these unreasonable people I would answer briefly as follows. I believe Christ more than the Fathers. If they say: But you do not believe the Fathers! Then I answer: And you do not believe Christ. But to reasonable people I answer in this way: We do not find that they actually called it a sacrifice, because they never sold it. The mother of Augustine begged her son to think of her with his prayer in the mass.[10] Yes indeed! I would ask for that, too. They administered it just as we do, except that they gave it the name sacrifice, which is taken from the Old Testament. That is, when the people came and brought gifts and gave them to the priests, they called it a sacrifice. This custom remained with the Christians, as is made clear from the words of the apostle: "When you come together to eat, wait for one another" (1 Cor. 11:33). This was a sacrificial meal. For the first Christians did not have wine and bread in the sacristy but instead brought together a lot of bread and wine. The priest took bread that he wanted to sacrifice and lifted it up. That was called a "collect," or a collection, and what was left over of bread and wine he gave to the poor. That they called it a sacrifice is merely a vestige from the Old Testament.[11] In Hebrew *missa* means "tax," especially inheritance tax. This is what the Jews called the tax that they brought to the priests. Not that the Christians regarded it as a sacrifice and wanted to be reconciled to God by it, but as Ambrose says: I receive the Sacrament daily, just as the blood of Christ, which once had been shed on the cross, is distributed daily.[12]

In the same way, the term "priest" is retained for those who preach and administer the sacraments, although it is a term common to all Christians.[13] In the New Testament many such terms are retained like the garments and the temple, although it is not the same temple as in the Old Testament. For this reason one must not do what the papists want because of the word "sacrifice." Today our Lord God has no temple. Instead in the New Testament, the temple is where God's Word is preached. It is profitable for us to have such a common house. But we should no longer serve God in them as in the Old Testament. Nevertheless, even now the papists stand on it and cling to the term. Stone buildings and consecrations do not make a temple; they make a children's play-church.

I have mentioned this as an example that many terms are retained from the Old Testament. Thus the terms "priest" and "temple" are retained for special persons and places although they no longer befit our priests and temples alone but to all Christians and places which are defined by the word. So also the chasuble is from the Old Testament.[14] For this reason the following says nothing at all: The Fathers call the Sacrament a sacrifice; therefore it is a sacrifice. Rather Christ has abolished all sacrifices by the single sacrifice on the cross. The entire world should be full of sacrifices, as Zechariah 14:21 says.

Satan has destroyed the essence and the nature of the Sacrament through the fanatics, and the pope has taken away the one kind. Out of this has flowed the sea of errors. All this arises from the fact that the words of Christ are despised. The Sacrament is bread and wine comprehended in these words, "This is my body," "This is my blood." These words teach you that the Sacrament is to be administered in both kinds, that it is a divine promise, through which God gives you the true body in the bread and the true blood in the wine, and that it should be your own eternal gift and not shoved into heaven as the Enthusiasts do by saying: Christ sits at the right hand of God.

We will preach further about the true use, how we should enjoy it, and then urge you not to despise it.

Endnotes

[1]Luther is probably referring to such things as his own hymns on the parts of the catechism (LW 53:249–51, 271–73, and 277–81), his catechetical sermons (e.g., LW 51:133–93), his *Personal Prayer Book* (LW 43:3–45), and the original form of the Small Catechism itself, portions of which had been printed as early as January 1529 on single sheets of paper and sold individually. By 1529 both his *Personal Prayer Book* and the Small Catechism appeared with woodcuts illustrating the various commandments, articles, petitions, and sacraments.

[2] Luther attacks here the notion, prominent among medieval theologians, that the Sacrament is effective *ex opere operato*, that is, from the mere performance of the rite or action. This allowed the grace in the Supper to be applied to people not present or even the dead, and it restricted the importance of faith and God's promise. See *The Babylonian Captivity of the Church* (LW 36:19–57).

[3] Cf. Luther's attack from 1521 in *The Misuse of the Mass* (LW 36:162–948).

[4] That is, the command,"You take," is plural not singular.

[5] German: *Pfäfflein*. Luther uses the diminutive as a derogatory description of the Roman priests and their mass.

[6] Luther uses the scholastic terminology somewhat loosely here. Peter Lombard, building on distinctions made by Augustine in his struggles with the Donatists, distinguished between the sacraments of the Old and New Covenants. He argued that, while the sacraments of the Old (such as circumcision and temple sacrifices) were effective *ex opere operantis* (by the disposition or work of the one offering the sacrifices), those of the New contained a stronger grace and, hence, were effective *ex opere operato* (by the mere performance of the rite or action). Here Luther refers the latter to the presence of Christ in the Sacrament that brings grace and contrasts that to the work of the priest who performs the mass.

[7] See above, note 5.

[8] The following year, 1530, Luther expanded on this in his *Admonition concerning the Sacrament of the Body and Blood of Our Lord* (LW 38:124–37).

[9] See, for example, Augustine, *Confession*, IX.xi.27 (NPNF, series 1, 1:138), and Ambrose, bishop of Milan (ca. 339-97), *Two Books on the Decease of Satyrus*, II.5 & 46 (NPNF, series 2, 10:171 & 181).

[10] See above, note 9.

[11] The origins of the word "mass" are uncertain.

[12] The reference may be to Ambrose, *De sacramentis*, IV.6.28; cf. V.4.25.

[13] Luther is referring to the word *sacerdos*, used in the Old Testament for the temple priests but in the New only for Christ or, as in 1 Peter 2:9, for all Christians.

[14] This and other comments on the history of liturgy are not accurate.

Wednesday Morning, Holy Week
March 24, 1529
The Lord's Supper
Received by Faith in the Word

You have heard what the Sacrament is in itself and that through the Word it is made pure from all the errors the devil has set against it. As a result, you know that it is nothing other than a created element and God's Word added to it, that is, bread and wine with the Word. One should note this, because that is where the power is. For the devil prowls around trying to pervert the Sacrament and this Word for us.

We see this all the time! Just look at the pope and the fanatical spirits who play with the Sacrament! For this reason we must not lapse into a false sense of security.

Today we want to deal with the true use: how we should enjoy it and how we should approach the Sacrament. First of all, one must keep the body modest and sober; next, one must forget everything else, think only about how to receive the Sacrament, and not approach it like swine. These were the only preparations known in the papacy, through which people prepared themselves as if for a work. Such things are good in and of themselves. It is fine that the body be sober and reasonable. But it must be a truly natural, wholesome fasting. Fasting is a work of righteousness. But we have taught that those fasts, like the fasts of the monks, are nothing. But with this we have not discarded this other fasting, whereby the body is best prepared to receive the Sacrament. In the same way, we have rejected the prayer of the rosary, but not honest prayer. We have purified such prayer and not rejected it. As we have straightened out prayer, so also fasting.

The true preparation for this Sacrament consists of faith. There are two parts which you must believe. First, that bread and wine are the body and the blood of our Lord Jesus Christ. For the fanatical spirits rage against this part and will not have it be the true body and blood. This faith is based on the words, "This is my body," "This is my blood." Do not fool with this faith! It has been the best thing about the papacy that this faith was preserved, that they did not doubt that the body and the blood are present. Stick to the words!

Others have also given fine parables of this to rouse the simple people so that they understand it. I like these a lot—like that of the mirror:[1] If it shatters, it becomes many pieces. But however many pieces there are, each has the same face in it. This is a parable for the children. In this way the body of Christ could be in so many pieces of bread and yet the whole body remains. I do not despise such parables; they please me for the sake of the simple. But it would be a lot better for someone to cling to the Word and think about it, since it can not lie and stands the test. If you know Christ's words, you will be strong enough; for the words have the power to move a person.

I say this because the devil has again sown a new seed. When he sees that he cannot maintain his error, he says: If some people cannot believe that Christ's body and blood are present, certainly they won't be damned just because they can't believe or understand it. Thus the devil wants to make of the Sacrament something that need not be believed and says: The Lord's Supper is not dealt with in the Apostles' Creed, therefore it's not necessary to believe it! Watch out here! You also do not find the Ten Commandments, the Lord's Prayer, or Baptism in the Apostles' Creed. This is what the devil does to lead us astray. But you should not leave up in the air whether the Sacrament is true or not. Here not conditional but unconditional statements are valid.

Therefore you may not say: If the Sacrament is the body and blood of Christ, then I believe it; if not, I do not trouble my head about it. This is the devil's game, which he plays so that it appears as if he were not against the Sacrament. For this reason he says neither yes or no. But a yes or no must be said. You also would not tolerate it in your house, if whenever you told the farm hand to carry out the manure he would reply: If the master has ordered it, then I will do it! Much less will God and Christ tolerate our uncertainty or doubt about his Word and command. Therefore you should be so certain in all articles that you are more certain of them than of your own body and say: I believe with certainty that the body and blood of Christ are present, just as I am sure that God lives. This is now one part of going to the Sacrament in a worthy manner.

The pope has also diligently expressed this in canon law.[2] The story is told about a priest who doubted the Sacrament and did not want to believe that Christ's body and blood were contained in the bread and wine. But after he was instructed and had been taught from the words of Scripture, he came to faith and confessed: Now I know and believe so firmly that Christ's body and blood are present in this Sacrament, that I grind it with the teeth and with the tongue! You can therefore do nothing better than to accept the words and say: My Lord Christ, who does not lie, has said these words!

If you need a parable, then take this one. Observe that when the sun shines in a great lake or pond, then naturally there must be no more than a single image of the sun in the water, because there is only one sun. How does it happen, then, that if hundreds upon hundreds of people stand around the lake, all would have an image of the sun in front of them where they stood and at no other place? And if they go around the lake, then the picture would go with them and would be in all places where they went. And if a thousand eyes look into the water, then each would see the picture in front of him or her and not before someone else. Now then, the sun is a created thing, and in a certain way it can be in the lake at all points. Dear friend, who will make us deny that God can far more readily know and find a way by which Christ's one body can be present according to his will, everywhere or wherever he wishes?[3] But I want to stress the Word more so that one does not take the parables without the Word. This is the first part of a person's preparations, namely, to believe that the true body and blood of Christ are present.

But now in addition, a higher faith belongs to this and is more accurately called trust and is based on the words: "given for you," and "shed for you for the forgiveness of sins." These words are the promise. They promise something, as when a citizen says to his neighbor: I will give you my field! There is a promise, and in the promise a gift. Now where a promise is present and a gift is offered, trust belongs to this, that is: a heart believes that this will happen. Here are gifts of God that need a faith that relies on the promise.

Even the devils and all the papists have the first faith, that the true body and blood are present as the words state. Indeed this faith should be present, but this is not enough. The devil certainly believes that Christ is Lord over sin, death, and hell. But these words he cannot believe: "for you;" he is concerned for you; he is yours; he is given to you. To rely on this: that he is mine, truly mine, that Christ is not only *a* Lord, but *my* Lord—this is the one, true Christian faith and work of the Holy Spirit.

Likewise in our city, when a citizen therefore says: The Margrave is a lord, the King of Bohemia is a lord, this I believe. But such a one does not say my lord, for my lord is the Duke of Saxony.[4] I do not accept that one since I am not under his protection; only when I can add "mine" can I accept him. In the same way I can say: This is my neighbor's wife, but I cannot say: my wife, likewise my house, my money, my servant. For this reason I cannot count on any of them. If the "mine" is added, it is a different faith than without the "mine." In the same way here. If the faith is merely "this is Christ's body," it is still not enough. Rather it must be added that he should be yours and mine, that he gives his body and blood to me in the Sacrament, so that I should enjoy it. Then I can say: I will possess this body that is given to me at the altar, so that he is my treasure. Those words bring the treasure, and the faith, which clings to them, preserves it.

These words sound laughable in the ears of the Enthusiasts[5] who say: Where is this written that the people should receive the comfort of the forgiveness of sins in this Sacrament? Nowhere do I see that Christ commands us in this way or gives the forgiveness of sins and salvation in this way! Such people have fallen from the faith and from the Word into works and are blind with open eyes in that they do not see these words. With so many books written by me and with my zealous instruction, I have achieved nothing. When Christ says, "given for you," does that not indicate to us that the body is given for us? Would Christ have to add, if you receive it, you will have the forgiveness of sins? I should cling to those words, which God does not speak in vain nor to stones, statues, cows and dogs. They carry with themselves a promise—indeed are a promise—and state clearly that his body given for our sins shall be present. Indeed, they say, this has happened on the cross not in the Sacrament. Answer: I, too, know this, that Christ died and shed his blood for us on the cross. But here it stands contained in the words. If the forgiveness does not extend further than the three hours on the cross, then it is all done in one day and his suffering is no good for us.

But how is it imparted to us? Through faith. How do I acquire faith? Through the words. What words are these? You must know that my body and blood are given for you. These words speak of a work which happened once on one day. But the words have gone out from the beginning of the world up to its end, because forgiveness of sins is proclaimed through the Word that speaks of the work that happened on the cross. Innumerable deaths of Christ do us no good if the Word does not proclaim his death for us.

Our enemies get stuck in this work: Christ died on the cross, not in the Lord's Supper. Therefore the forgiveness of sins is on the cross, not in the Lord's Supper. But how do I acquire it? When I believe, they answer. They attach themselves to this last work on the cross. But then must faith be only in the place where Christ was crucified? One cannot come to faith if it is not preached, as Paul says: "And how are they to believe in one of whom they have never heard? And how are they to hear without someone to proclaim him?" (Romans 10:14). So if Christ were crucified a hundred times in a day and no one preached it, then the forgiveness of sins would be lost. For this reason the work completed on the cross must be contained in the Word and be offered to the people through the Word. It is a vexatious devil who wants to be deaf in such a malicious way. It vexes me. But you look to yourselves! We cannot comprehend it with our reason.

These words of Christ spoken at the last supper, which are now spoken at the altar are as much the Gospel as if I were to say in the pulpit: I proclaim to you that Christ has died for you. The words at the altar are the same: "Take, eat, drink, etc." Is this not Gospel? They run rough shod over the Word and do not want to hear that the simple word is Gospel! They do not want to see that Christ's gospel is bound to the wine and bread. They are words of the Gospel that speak of body and blood and offer us Christ's body and blood. But the devil knows well what is at stake in this. For this reason he tries to snatch us from the Word. Once he achieves this, no one can resist him. But you must say: Those words are the promise in which Christ offers me his body and blood, given for me. The redemption and forgiveness of sins happened on the cross. But it must be proclaimed so that I may hear it. I will never experience it by simply looking at the cross. At the time many stood at the cross but they did not know that there forgiveness of sins would be gained until the voice came and directed them to the cross. If you take away the word "for you" from the cross, you see Christ as a thief on the gallows. But the words must teach you that he is the Savior.

For this reason stick with the words; for Satan knows well that it is his business to snatch you from them. If these words remain, then the Sacrament also remains pure and he can do nothing to us. This is the true faith and the proper preparation for the Sacrament: that your heart clings to the Word of Christ. Therefore you should think: I am also in the group to whom this Word is spoken. It offers to those who come to him the body and blood of Christ given for them, and it preaches to them that on the cross Christ's body was given for them and Christ's blood was shed for them. On this basis we say that in the Sacrament is forgiveness of sins, comfort, and strength for faith; for there is the Gospel that proclaims the forgiveness of sins. Therefore you have to ground yourself in these words: "given for you."

Though some would translate the text "shed for you" as "poured out for you," yet what follows, "for the forgiveness of sins," remains true. This is not an unimportant word, for here lies the treasure. In the Apostles' Creed you say nothing more than "I believe ... in the forgiveness of sins," and you hear these same words in the Sacrament. If there were nothing other than this word "forgiveness of sins," it would be enough. When God speaks of the forgiveness of sins together with the body and blood that he gives, we should depend on it.

Where God promises something and says, "I will do this for you," that is where faith belongs. With every promise faith is required. For this reason I say that such a faith belongs to the Sacrament, that the body and blood is your food given for the forgiveness of sins, and when you receive the body and blood you receive a treasure and a gift given for your sins. When you eat it, then believe that it is Christ's body given to you for the forgiveness of sins. It could not be said more clearly. The only thing missing is that no one looks at the text.

Now you have the true use of the Sacrament. It may be enjoyed in no other way than in faith, that both Christ's body and blood and the forgiveness of sins are present. When you receive it, you should be certain: you have received the seal that God will forgive your sins.

This is a different use than under the pope. Previously I thought that by receiving the Sacrament I had done a work through which I would be saved. Therefore one made an idol of the Sacrament. It is no compulsion and law. As I have said of confession,[6] learn also of the Sacrament. One preaches on the sacraments and on confession so that the people may learn what they are. When you perceive your sin, you will come voluntarily and will compel us to administer it. Your sins will indeed drive you to compel and force us. Simply put the words in front of you: "This is my body, given for you," "This is my blood, shed for you." When you truly believe these words, you will come and compel us to give it to you because you realize that the Sacrament is a treasure. Therefore the pope should drop the law and compulsion for those who receive the Sacrament.[7] Instead he does the opposite. However, you should learn what the Sacrament is and what God offers in it, and then you will come of your own accord.

A twofold faith is necessary. The first part believes that the words, "This is my body," "This is my blood," are true. The second part believes that both are given for you, that you have the forgiveness of sins that brings righteousness and eternal life. The one faith says: This is Christ's body. The other: This body is mine. Do not come forward without this faith! You must have this faith or at least ask for it.

Now you know what the Sacrament is and how you should use it. The exhortation is yet to come. We will save it for tomorrow.

Endnotes

[1] This illustration was also used in Luther's *Confession concerning Christ's Supper* of 1528 (LW 37:226).

[2] This portion of Roman Canon Law (Gratian, *Decretum* Pt. III, *De consecratione*, d. 2, c. 42), was first cited in opposition to the real presence by Ulrich Zwingli in his *Commentary on True and False Religion*, trans. & ed. by S. M. Jackson & C. N. Heller (Philadelphia: Heidelberg Press, 1929; Reprint: Durham, NC: Labyrinth Press, 1981), 210. In his *Confession concerning Christ's Supper* (LW 37:300f.) Luther defended this confession of Berengar of Tours (ca. 998–1088).

[3] This illustration was also used in Luther's *Confession concerning Christ's Supper* (LW 37:277).

[4] Wittenberg was part of Electoral Saxony. Its prince was the Elector John.

[5] German: *Schwärmer*. For a definition see above, p. 62 note 3. For this argument see Ulrich Zwingli, *Commentary on True and False Religion*, 228.

[6] See above, p. 41f.

[7] See above, p. 45 note 9.

Maundy Thursday Morning
March 25, 1529
An Exhortation
to Receive the Lord's Supper

Thus far in four days you have heard the correct understanding and teaching concerning this revered Sacrament. I hope that now you have understood what the Sacrament is and therefore have an ample understanding against all fanatics and errors. Satan has given rise to all sorts of fanatics, prowling around the Word, who would like to snatch it away from us. The Sacrament is bread and wine, yet bound to the Word: "This is my body," "This is my blood." This is what was said about the teaching.

Now we come to the exhortation.[1] For I see well how remiss you are in availing yourselves of the Sacrament. Some say no one should approach who is not hungry, that is, no one should go to it unless driven by his or her sins. Others say they have no need of it. Satan has often kept me from the Sacrament, too.

You have a clear text in which the Lord says at both places, "Do this in remembrance of me." Seize it zealously! You see that these words command something of us and that Christ imposes on those who want to be Christians to approach the Sacrament because he said, "Do this." This is required, and I am obliged to do it. The text has even tormented the papists so that the people do not know what they should do. Thereupon they said that the Lord spoke to the whole group, so that it is enough if a few do it. Just as if it were said: The Wittenbergers should go out and work on the moat.[2] If a few do it, then it is enough! Therefore, when Christ says, "Do this in remembrance of me," it is enough if only those consecrated by the pope do it. Thus we continually make the words a wax nose[3] and twist them to accord with our way of thinking. But let the Word apply to those with whom Christ speaks! He speaks with his disciples and commands them to eat and drink. He does not say to one group "Take and eat," and to another "Do this in remembrance of me!" You have two reasons to go to the Sacrament. The first is the text; the second is your need.

But, they object, Christ says "as often as you drink it." There he is not compelling me, but leaves it up to my free choice. That's true. But the text does not say that you should never do it. When he says "as often," then it should happen often. It is implied in them that one should do it often as the words clearly show. But he tacks on the phrase "as often" because he wants to keep this Sacrament voluntary. It is not like the Jews who have to celebrate their Passover on the fourteenth day of the month in April or March as the case may be. We are free from having to keep the full moon of March or April.

But we have Passover on all Sundays, indeed on all days, as if Christ would say: I impose on you a Passover which you are to do often throughout the year, when and where you want. I bind you in no time or place as the papists have bound the people to this day.[4] Therefore this Word is a command that does not give you the freedom to stay away from the Sacrament or to go only once in six years. I say this not only to the laity, but also to "brother studium" and the teachers.[5] Christ wants a person to do this, with the proviso that it be voluntary. He does not specify a certain place but leaves it up to your discretion.

Secondly, Christ says: If you want to do it, then do it to remember me. The Old Testament Passover will no longer be preached. Henceforth the remembrance of the miracles and the exodus from Egypt should not be kept. Instead you shall celebrate what I have done, as at one time they preached about the exodus from Egypt.

This is the chief exhortation. Those not touched by this will not be moved at all. Even if I had no need, it would certainly be enough that Christ says, "Do this in remembrance of me." I do not compel you to go to the Sacrament on Easter or Pentecost, but still this text stands so firm so that you should not despise the Sacrament, refuse to yearn for it, or construct for yourself a fleshly freedom as if the Sacrament were not necessary. Therefore you are not free to despise it. But you certainly do despise it if, while capable of doing other works and not too weak to go to the Sacrament, you let yourself be hindered from this work and neglect it. Ask yourself whether you, too, are a Christian, whether you yearn for what Christ has commanded his disciples.

If you discontinue going to the Sacrament, then you become cold and lax. I have experienced this myself and you also will experience how your love and your heart become cold and how you stand with God. However, whoever draws near must remember the commands and words of God. From this you acquire other thoughts that turn you to the Lord. But you go seven years and do not care how you stand with God because you do not take the time to consider such things! But if you would draw near, your heart would be renewed. The Lord knows well that we are such irresponsible and cold fellows.

For this reason the Sacrament is tied to a command that we should receive it, not at definite times and places, but that we should strive to draw near frequently and think of the Lord. For he wants us to think of him and not forget. Otherwise his remembrance would certainly soon die out. When people hear God's Word in public preaching, they are not so greatly moved as when they draw near to the altar; for there the word of the priest relates to their own person. Let this be said to you who want to be true Christians, that you do not act so nonchalant about it. This is the one reason that should move us often to the Sacrament, namely, Christ's command that has indeed set us free from time and place, but not from refraining to take it altogether.

But then a person makes an excuse: Indeed, I am not worthy of it. This is my temptation too. You heard in the papists' sermons that we should be entirely pure and without blemish when coming to the Sacrament. It made us so anxious and despairing as a result, that immediately the thought came into the heart: I am not worthy. If the heart tries to compare our worthiness with Christ's, they appear together like filth and gold. I see my filth over against Christ's righteousness. Then a person says, I will wait until tomorrow or until a Sunday when I am deserving or more worthy. The Sunday waits for one, for two years: One Sunday brings another; a quarter year, a half year; an entire year, a second year. This comes from the old nature. If I intend to go only when I am entirely pure and nothing afflicts my conscience, then I will never go to the Sacrament. Whenever I ought to be completely righteous, Satan will come and ruin this excellent work, so that I will never achieve it.

Here distinguish the impudent people who are publicly involved in adultery, usury, oppression, theft, hatred or envy. Such hard, unrefined, wild people may be told not to come to the Sacrament. For they are not worthy to receive the forgiveness of sins, and want to remain evil. Throw them out! Such people are unworthy who live in public shame and blasphemy. St. Hilary said: "Unless people commit a sin that is just cause to remove them from the community and regard them as non-Christians, they should not stay away from the Sacrament, lest they be deprived of life."[6] We should not get in the habit of distancing ourselves from the Sacrament, as certainly happens to those who allow nothing to move them.

Therefore if your sins are not the kind for which the Christian church would be likely to punish you openly, you should not let yourself be removed from the Sacrament nor should you be prevented from going to it. You should say: I come not on my worthiness, or else I could never come. Even a child is not brought to baptism because she or he is righteous. In the same way I do not come to confession based on my purity. Now no one should confess who does not desire to lay hold of grace, but all who would like comfort, would desire grace, and would like to become righteous, let them go to Baptism, to the Sacrament, and to confession. Therefore they alone are unworthy who, like the Corinthians [1 Corinthians 11:17–34], afflict and despise one another.

I, too, am just now learning to comprehend that access to the Sacrament is not based on our worthiness, but that instead I come as an unworthy person who cannot be worthy. God protect me from my worthiness! Indeed I would like to be worthy, but that is an art which I cannot achieve. For this reason I come standing on your Word, O God, and I seek holiness and righteousness from you. In this way the proud nature is driven out. There a person throws away his or her own works and worthiness and clings to God. This is one thing which makes you worthy. It is difficult to do. It is also the case with prayer. You think: I would indeed like to pray, but I am not worthy. Therefore we look more and more to our hands than to Christ's mouth although we should say: I look to what you say, not to what I do.

The second thing that should move us is the promise, about which you have heard the entire week. Christ's promise "for you" is even stronger than the command. Whoever is not moved by this ought not go to the Sacrament. If you will be a Christian and a disciple of Christ, then you have his command to approach apart from your worthiness or unworthiness. Next comes the promise to me: "Do this in remembrance of me," and "Take, eat and drink." This is sheer comfort, offered to distressed people who would like the forgiveness of sins. Note both parts well! First of all, you are driven by the command, and second, lay hold of his promise in order to draw near. For God has not set down poison for us, that we should eat our death (if you do not make it a poison for yourself), but instead it is a precious medicine and food that helps you in soul and body and gives to you eternal life in soul and body. Therefore it is not a poison.

But to those who lead depraved, wild lives everything is poison; there is nothing on earth that does not become poison and harm to them. But those who wish to be considered in the number of Christians should consider that the Sacrament is not a poison but a remedy and a nourishment, spiritually and bodily. For if it goes well with the soul, then it also goes well with the body. Your reception of the Sacrament is based on the mouth of the Lord who has commanded and promised it. He does not wish to give something bad but instead gives the forgiveness of sins.

Do you not know what the forgiveness of sins is? When you have the forgiveness of sins, there is God's grace and mercy and the Holy Spirit, redemption from death against devil, world and flesh. In conclusion: Through the command "Do this in remembrance of me," you are urged, and through the promise of the forgiveness of sin you are coaxed to go to the Sacrament, whether you are worthy or not. If you are unworthy, then ask God: Make me worthy!

Furthermore you have not only God's Word, command and promise, but also your need around your neck. The Lord sees this and says: "Come to me all you that are weary and carrying heavy burdens, and I will give you rest" (Matthew 11:28). Am I addressing the saints and the wise? They have no need of the medicine. But indeed I call to you who are weary and carrying heavy burdens. Are you heavy laden with sins, the fear of death, greediness, temptation of the flesh and the like, then you are burdened. Where will you go? Bid farewell to those who say: I will wait until I have become free and refreshed, then I will come to you! Then you would not need me nor I you. But you will find much in your heart that afflicts you. Christ sees this. For this reason he institutes the Sacrament, commands it, and bases it on his Word so that you may have a means against such afflictions.

But suppose you say: How am I to do it? I feel neither hunger nor thirst nor encumbrance, and you want those who are burdened! For this reason I will wait until I feel this way! But take care not to wait too long! To those who feel no encumbrance, I advise that they grab on to their breast and feel whether they also have blood and flesh. Then, if you feel this, go to Paul's Epistle to the Romans (1:29ff.) and to Galatians and read what are the fruits of the flesh: "adultery, fornication, impurity, licentiousness, idolatry, sorcery, enmities, strife, jealousy, anger, quarrels, dissensions, factions, envy, murder,[7] drunkenness, carousing and things like these" (Galatians 5:19–21).

But, you say: I feel nothing of these fruits in me! Then look more carefully! If you are still blind, then believe the Scripture which knows your flesh better than you yourself. When Paul ventures to say of his flesh, "I know that nothing good dwells within me, that is, in my flesh" (Romans 7:18), and you do not feel it, it is all the more troubling and is a sign that your flesh is leprous and dead and feels nothing. If you rightly felt your flesh, you would be speaking differently. If you do not feel it, then believe God's Word and consider: I am flesh and blood and certainly do not do what pleases God. The flesh hinders everything good and all knowledge of God and of Christ. If you do not feel it, you still have two reasons to come to the Sacrament, just like one who is ill but does not want to admit it, who either lets the doctor in or does not.

The Scripture is more truthful than you are. It says there is nothing good in your flesh and that the flesh struggles against the Spirit. If you do not feel the flesh in your breast but only wood and stone, then blame St. Paul for lying.

In the same way, since you are in the world, you will also not be lacking sins. If you want to grasp the truth and hold it fast, immediately you will have enemies who trouble you, are hostile to you, and will not allow you one piece of bread. Then wait and see whether you will not be angry and curse. If you do not know that you are in the world, then take a look at yourself as you live among your neighbors! But if you don't believe yourself, then believe the Scripture which says, "The whole world lies under the power of the evil one" (1 John 5:19) and "for all that is in the world—the desire of the flesh, the desire of the eyes, the pride in riches—comes not from the Father, but from the world" (1 John 2:16). As the flesh is against the Spirit, so, too, is the world.

In the same way you are under the devil. All the apostles were under him, especially because of the flesh. The devil comes after you unceasingly to lead you astray, poison the air, and take everything from you. Thus the devil has many spears aimed at you. When you recognize them, be glad that you are able to go to the Sacrament. But because you are not concerned about him, you despise the Sacrament.

In confession, in the Sacrament, and in Baptism, the Word is directed especially to us. The need is there. First of all, you are stuck in sin. You may read this in Galatians (5:19) and Romans (7:18). But you say: I would like to go to the Sacrament, but afterwards my flesh does not want to. It wants to grope around and feel, but not believe. If you do not feel it, then you are doubly ill: you have flesh, and this flesh is leprous. Then say to the priest: I confess to you my need so that it does not penetrate to my heart. For this reason I ask that you comfort me, pray for me, that the stone and log be taken from my heart. But when you finally discover you are stuck in it twice as deeply as any other sinner, do not say: I am unworthy; for this reason I will not go to the Sacrament!

You truly need it! Otherwise you will be stuck not only in sin but in great danger besides. For Satan continually tries to seduce you with lies into a false faith. He is a liar "prowling around like a roaring lion looking for someone to devour" (1 Peter 5:8). He certainly does this to me. But if he is so far from you that he does not attack you, this is not good. In that case say to yourself: I have twice the evil. Others complain about the wickedness of the devil, that he will not allow them to remain in the pure Word and faith. I do not feel this. For this reason, you pastors, help me and pray for me! I am one of those about whom Christ speaks, "Come to me all you that are weary and carrying heavy burdens!" (Matt. 11:28), and I am doubly burdened. I know that I am a sinner and stand in danger of the devil's attacks. Therefore I believe the devil has caused my lack of feeling, because the Lord wants to give grace through the Sacrament, so that I feel my burden.

Beyond this, you see that the devil is a murderer. You are not safe for one hour even to joke about this. He drowns you in the water; another makes it to shore and breaks his neck. But I do not feel his presence. Neither did those who drowned in the Elbe![8] If the devil was around Peter, Paul, and Christ, he will also certainly be around you. And this is a double evil when you are in such danger and are not aware of it. But those who are aware of their sins and the desires of the flesh and their heart's fierce envy, dwell in a flesh that is not dead and leprous but still feels and lives. They should go to the Sacrament and say: I am in sin, in the world, and under the power of the devil. O Lord, help me! But if you do not believe this, then listen to Peter, "Your adversary the devil prowls around, looking for someone to devour" (1 Peter 5:8). Believe Peter; he has felt the devil and survived his activity. Do not ignore the devil or, before you know it, he will chop off your head.

For this reason, because Christ saw all this, he commanded us to pray and instituted the Sacrament for us to administer often, so that we are protected against the devil, world, and flesh. When the devil attacks, come for strength to the dear Word so that you may know Christ and long for the Sacrament! A soldier has his rations and must have food and drink to be strong. In the same way here: those who want to be Christians should not throw the Sacrament to the winds as if they did not need it.

There is immeasurable need for it. You have three enemies against you: the world, the flesh, the devil. They do not take a holiday. They do not rest until you cheat your neighbor. And you sit there like a log and are completely unaware of your sins. But, you say, I do not feel it. Then listen to what the Holy Spirit says: "In my flesh is nothing good" (Romans 7:18). Now what do you think is in your flesh, to make you such a hardened person? The devil hovers over you; the world and the flesh do not take a holiday. A hundred thousand sins and death stand around you; all stones, water, and fire, all hours are full of death. Every bite you eat, everything you drink, every rope and stair is a danger to your life. To whom should we turn? To Christ! Then a different thought will arise so that you say: I do not feel sin, world, death, devil and yet I am under them. Give me grace, that I may be otherwise!

First of all it is commanded that you go to the Sacrament; then there are promised comfort and salvation. Do not wait two long years! With God's help overcome the temptation to wait one Sunday and then another and another! Say instead: Whoever is not worthy today will be even less so tomorrow.

Endnotes

[1] This exhortation is the basis for the ones in the Small and Large Catechisms. See BC, Small Catechism, Preface, 21–25, and Large Catechism, Lord's Supper, 38–84.

[2] At the time Wittenberg was strongly fortified. It was the duty of citizens to contribute to the repairs of the walls. Two years later Luther sent a blistering letter to Duke John complaining about the Duke's bailiff in Wittenberg, John Metzsch, who refused to repair the walls (LW 50:23–26).

[3] This metaphor for willful interpretation of the Bible was common among the scholars of Luther's day.

[4] See above, p. 45 note 9.

[5] Expression from student's slang. Luther was speaking to the University students.

[6] Here Luther depends on Gratian, *Decretum*, Pt. III, d. 2, c. 15, who attributes this citation to Hilary. In fact it comes from Augustine, *Epistle* 54.3 (NPNF, series 1, 1:300f.).

[7] The NRSV and most modern translations omit the word "murder."

[8] The river that flows next to Wittenberg.

Maundy Thursday Afternoon
March 25, 1529
The Passion: Anointing in Bethany, Last Supper, and Footwashing

We have proposed to preach on the Passion of Christ over three days and not, as was done in the past, for eight hours straight. Instead we want to divide it up over five hours. We do this so that the Passion story might continue to be known among the laity. I will simply read the text condensed from the four gospels,[1] because for the rest of the year, you hear sermons on Wednesdays and Saturdays devoted to the two Evangelists (Matthew and John), where all of these texts are interpreted at a slower pace. For this reason, this is to be a simple sermon, in which we will read the text.

This morning I admonished you that on account of God's command and promise and our need, we should not despise the Sacrament. I urge not only you older folks, but also the young, to cling to the 10 Commandments, the Creed, and the Lord's Prayer. This has already happened with us older folks. Now the children must be instructed and recite before the deacons what they have learned at home. They are to be held to the command to "Do this in remembrance of me," so that they also participate in the Sacrament with us and pray with us.

Now the festival of Unleavened Bread, which is called the Passover, was near" (Luke 22:1). In the Old Testament, during this time no one had leavened bread, but had bread similar to our communion wafers.

"Then the chief priests and the scribes[2] and the elders of the people gathered" [Matthew 26:3]. The Evangelists indicate three kinds of fanatics that attacked Christ. The first were the Pharisees. There was no more honored position under the law, but they were mixed in among the chief priests and scribes. The elders were the councilors of the city Jerusalem; indeed this was a glorious thing to be. In Peter the elders are called councilors and regents. A threefold authority existed in Jerusalem: the Roman, the municipal, and the levitical. For in addition to the Roman, they had their own civic authority, which was divided into two parts: an earthly and a spiritual authority. And the scribes were, as in our time, preachers, who had the authority to remove or install clergy. But a councilor in Jerusalem indeed had as much authority as a lesser prince to us. They had great power and authority and a great number of people subordinate to them. These assembled in order to deliberate how they should seize Jesus, not with raw power, but with cunning.

Moreover they would not do it on the festival, for the people had come to Jerusalem from as far away as 700 miles. They had come from all parts of the Roman Empire, which numbered three million men, not counting women and children. I do not know whether in all Germany there is so great a number of people.[3] For this reason they said: "Consider that the entire people gape at him! We must use cunning and choose the right time, so that our cunning succeeds." Evil people never lack the will.

"While he was at Bethany in the house of Simon the leper, as he sat at the table, a woman came with an alabaster jar of very costly ointment of nard" [Mark 14:3]. The Lord entertains nothing but thoughts of death. "After two days the Passover is coming" (Matt. 26:2) means "my life is on the line." When Mary poured out the ointment, he interpreted it concerning his death: "By pouring this ointment on my body she has prepared me for burial." [Matthew 26:12]. Other people's bodies are anointed after death but I before death while still alive. He makes such a precious work from what Mary has done. In conclusion: a good tree brings forth good fruit.

The ointment was a water, not an oil and bath ointment as the barber uses, but a precious, delicate water, like the balm used for anointing a king or priest. There one would not pour an ointment over them like our ointments, but a precious ointment that would have had a precious aroma. It was a fine, sweet water that one could sprinkle over oneself like rosewater, endive water, nard, spike, lavender, a precious spike or lavender water to us. Nevertheless it had this difference. For with us there is nothing compared to that found in warmer regions. They call it an ointment, it may have been in a glass or a stone jar. It certainly had a pleasing smell as John (12:3) writes. If it had been a bath ointment, then it would have damaged the head and clothes. It had a value of 300 pfennig, worth one to six gulden. This happened in the evening.

"Then Satan entered into Judas" [Luke 22:3]. Then once more the chief priests and the authorities are named. Judas went to them and put Christ up for sale. He did not let himself be summoned or sought after but comes on his own. He had long prepared the meal, now it had been cooked. There would be much to preach about. Judas still goes into the world and produces grief.

"Where do you want us to make the preparations for you to eat the Passover?" [Matthew 26:17]. We have already dealt with this text. Luke [22:17, 20] describes with greatest care that Christ gave the cup twice. For the last time he gave them a "farewell drink." This was a cup of pure wine and a "farewell drink" to signal that he would no longer drink wine on earth. Therefore he discharged the old Passover and his old life. One must note such things against the Enthusiasts,[4] that when he gives the farewell drink, he does not say, "This is my blood," but it was a farewell drink in which he says, "I tell you that from now on I will not drink of the fruit of the vine until the kingdom of God comes" [Luke 22:18]. There Christ attests that it shall be his farewell drink. And only Luke records this, so that we realize there are two different cups and that Jesus calls the first of these the "fruit of the vine."

If Christ's word is true, as it surely is, then the second cup is not the "fruit of the vine." Luke has with great care included these words, "I will no longer drink of wine." And he calls it not only wine but the "fruit of the vine," that is, whatever may be made from the vine.

Therefore the second cup must be something other than wine grown on the vine, namely Christ's blood. For this reason the first cup is to be strongly distinguished from the second. In the coming kingdom we, too, will drink.

The footwashing follows [John 13:1–11].[5] There you see that the Lord speaks as one who will depart and commands them with word and deeds to love and to serve one another. For this is the nature of love that it serves. For this reason he says, "By this everyone will know that you are my disciples" [John 13:35]. This was his final command. It is therefore true that one serves what one loves, as Christ himself did. Thus the one who hoards gold becomes its servant, and a father who loves his children shows them sheer service. Therefore Christ has thrown down all commands and given love alone as the final command: O dear disciples, I will not give you many commands, laws, and books. Love alone will teach you well what you should do. "Love one another just as I have loved you" [John 13:34]. I am your servant. This is the "example" [John 13:15], that he washes their feet. This is to be "the new commandment."

The very same commandment was present before this, but now Christ wants to push the others aside and only hold on to this one. Before I teach a mother what she should do for her child she already has done it. Her heart knows more than all books can write and preach. Such is a mother's love. Therefore Christ wants us to serve one another.

He said this especially to his disciples and added the horrible case of Judas to this, so that it should remain fresh in the memory of pastors and preachers. For the case of Judas should be an example to them to humble themselves.

First of all the Evangelist says: "Jesus got up from the table, took off his outer robe and tied a towel around himself. Then he poured water into a basin and began to wash his disciples' feet" [John 13:4f.]. There you see what kind of man he was. This must have been a dear companionship and such a happy life as we cannot begin to imagine it. This he has done as an example as he says, "You call me Teacher and Lord—and you are right, for that is what I am. So if I, your Lord and Teacher, have washed your feet, you also ought to wash one another's feet" [John 13:13f.]. This example is placed for Christians next to the teaching that they love and serve one another. For in the future they should be apostles and preachers and noble people. For the Gospel makes them teachers and their wisdom should hold true for the righteous and believers, although the world stands against it. However, since there is no more dangerous thing than to be proud in spiritual goods, with his humility Christ offers an example and secondly points out the horrible case of Judas.

Still it has helped nothing! It is incongruous that Christ should wash the feet of the disciples and the pope allows his feet to be kissed.[6] Indeed we should kiss one another's feet. I want to have nothing to do with having the special privilege whereby others kiss my feet and I do not also kiss theirs.

Christ saw what would happen. Indeed he saw that the successors of the apostles would be such people who allow themselves alone to be served but no longer serve themselves. Certainly it is said to all of us Christians, but above all to those who are successors of the apostles: they should serve one another.

This has to do not only with footwashing, although I would like it if one observed the custom especially when friends come, as one still preserves the custom in the monasteries and collegiate churches. But I would like the theatrical, pretentious footwashing to be banned. For it is pride pure and simple. I thought if I did it, I would be saved. If it had been done properly, as Christ did it, it would not be as in the monastery where a monk only washes the feet of another monk. Do you want to carry out Christ's example? Then wash the feet of a poor beggar who comes to you, give him food and a bed, and attend to him! Yes, this is our responsibility! Therefore Satan always produces hypocrisy and perverts Christ's works. For this reason I would like us to wash the feet of strangers, and especially those who come from far away. But even if we do not do this, we should still serve others according to this example.

"So if I, your Lord and Teacher, have washed your feet, you also ought to wash one another's feet," says the Lord and gives the following reason: "Servants are not greater than their master nor are the messengers greater than the one who sent them" [John 13:16]. If I am your Lord and send you, you should not be greater than I am. When I pour out water and wash your feet, do not feel ashamed of it. In conclusion: Wherever Christians are, they should be ready to serve another.

This is the Christian standard (the worldly standard is different), that I should regard my Christian neighbors as my lords and serve them in everything. It is true, great villainy would occur under this pretext.[7] For this reason I have said that I cannot institute it, because many godless people abuse our love. It cannot take place here as it did among early Christians. If one of them came from another city, he or she had a letter of testimony. If I or a pastor would begin it here—O what rogues we have!—then we would give food and drink and furnish them a bed. Many rascals would take advantage of it because we would not know which are righteous and which are godless. We must have prior acquaintance with them in order to serve one another. Just look what has happened in the well-to-do pilgrim hospices on the Rhine! They were established with the best of intentions, but the most wicked scoundrels abused them. You innkeepers don't care whom you have for guests. How then are we to do it? The Romans had a rule that not even one mouse could stir without permission.

But with us the land is full of rogues. No one pays attention to the kind of guests he has. For this reason I don't trust myself to institute this even though I would only set it up among our fellow citizens who are known to us. We would not want to become involved with unknown strangers, for we already have been deceived sufficiently by godless people in this city, who under the pretext of the Christian name begged from us and have abused our generosity. For this reason Christ says: "to one another" [John 13:14], not to each one who comes to town. Otherwise he would have said, let one be the servant of another. See in what a friendly manner the Lord attracts us to the Christian estate so that we should be happy to be Christians!

Christ saw clearly that if one should preach the Gospel then it will require that you put all your goods at risk, because the Gospel costs so much that Christians cannot be certain of their lives. Because it is difficult to be a Christian, Christ says: I will not leave you disconsolate. I will not forsake you. For one house I will give you all houses of all Christians. I will also give just as many Christians to serve you. All houses ought to be open to us, and our brothers and sisters ought to give us one hundred lives for one life.

Therefore if one keeps this commandment, would it not be a fine life? I know this in truth: If I am a Christian, I am lord of all Christians and on the other hand a servant of those who will receive me.[8] This means to receive a hundred houses for one as the Gospel says, "Everyone who has left houses or brothers or sisters or father or mother or fields, for my name's sake, will receive a hundredfold, and will inherit eternal life" (Matthew 19:29). If I am a Christian then Christ cares about me, and where others are Christians, they will not forsake me either. Likewise I must be so disposed to serve everyone as long as they are known to me.

It was necessary for Christ to leave behind an example to Christianity and to act in this way at his departure from this world. This should move us more than all other words. It is a horrible thing when a priest is proud. The Gospel, which should make hearts humble, now makes them proud, so that they want to rule over both kings and peasants. This is an abuse of the Gospel. This Christ had foreseen. For this reason he included the example of the footwashing and the horrible case of Judas. That evildoer lets himself be served and takes everything. But Christ wanted even Judas at his Last Supper so that people may know the horrible things that will happen to them. Such types are among our people, just as Judas was among the apostles.

Endnotes

[1] Luther used John Bugenhagen's *Synopsis of the Passion Narrative*, first published in Wittenberg in 1524.

[2] The NRSV and most modern translations omit the phrase "and the scribes."

[3] Mülhaupt, p. 76 note 16, estimates that the population of Germany around 1500 was between 13–14 million people.

[4] See above, page 59 note 3. Ulrich Zwingli argued in "On the Lord's Supper," [*Zwingli and Bullinger*, trans. G. W. Bromiley (Philadelphia: Westminster Press, 1953), 227] that this text proved the cup was not Chirst's blood.

[5] Rörer's notes indicate that Luther closely followed Bugenhagen's "Passion History" and read the entire chapter and attached the text of Luke 22 about the dispute among the disciples of who was the greater; further: "Now the Son of Man has been glorified" [John 13:31–38], "When once you have turned back, strengthen your brothers" [Luke 22:32], "I am ready to go with you to prison and to death!" [Luke 22:33–34], "When I sent you out without a purse" [Luke 22:35–38], and "Do not let your hearts be troubled" [John 14:1–27].

[6] This act of obeisance was practiced in the church of Luther's day.

[7] In what follows Luther reflects on the problem of distinguishing professional, religious beggars from the truly needy.

[8] This insight, central to Luther's understanding of Christian freedom, is also stated in *The Freedom of a Christian* (LW 31:344).

Good Friday Morning
March 26, 1529
The Passion: Gethsemane

Yesterday you heard about the Last Supper and the footwashing by the Lord. Today we shall hear of his Passion. But in order to consider it in a worthy manner, we want to preface it with an exhortation.

In the Passion of Christ all wisdom and pertinent pieces have been written for our instruction. These things were not heretofore dealt with when one used to preach on the Passion. Instead of these things they worked at moving old women to tears and even to pointing out the wickedness of the Jews. But that is not the main point. Rather one should consider the prophecies of the holy prophets, especially Isaiah, that the Passion of Christ is a punishment for our sins. And this is what one should consider and emphasize continuously.

For you have heard that all people are inclined to build on their own works and to make themselves righteous. The world is so deeply mired in this that it persecutes the Gospel. Then those who suffer much think they deserve much on that account. From this came the orders of monks. Many have taught about suffering and patience so as to preach it as the upright conduct by which to become righteous. In this they have twisted the word: "The rod and reproof give wisdom" [Prov. 29:15] and make righteous children. One tumbles quickly into that way of thinking, which is very deeply rooted in the human heart. If sin is abolished by self-torture, then one runs to St. James and another dons the cowl of a monk. Finally it came to this, that the priests taught the thieves and criminals to trust in their own death! In Christianity one should have preached that this is untrue. Instead the opposite was preached. Indeed, people preached a lot about Christ's suffering, but they exalted in their own suffering.

Therefore make a distinction between the suffering of Christ and our suffering, just as one must make a distinction between the work of Christ and our works, between those by which we should serve our neighbor and that through which we become righteous. Our works should remain on earth. We become righteous by faith alone. This demolishes all the monasteries, which have transferred to works what belongs to faith alone. In the same way, make a distinction between the suffering of Christ and our suffering. Let it be great as you want, whether the suffering of a thief or of someone sick with the plague, put all human suffering in a heap and say: All this suffering is not able to atone for one day's sin. This is easily said. But nothing has been preached more than suffering and patience. They said: If you endure suffering, then you are patient and will have the forgiveness of sins. However, they have not noticed that these are all our works.

So then one must give an answer to such sayings, as "The rod makes righteous children" and "Whoever is tortured must become righteous." To be sure, these are true in the household and in the city, here on earth, in bodily and outwardly ways, as when a child is outwardly chastised. Therefore tear down all these sayings, do not lift them up before God as if they could make one righteous! For this reason all monks with their cowls ask: should I not climb up higher than a chastened child or a servant in the house? If punishment and suffering could make one righteous, the devil and the most wicked evil-doer would long since have been righteous! But, they reply, what if such persons suffer and in addition do it gladly for God's sake? For this reason it pleased them to preach our own suffering as a necessary thing. No one realizes how deeply rooted in our nature it is to exalt our own suffering. Accordingly the venomous preachers stressed that.

Then when they hear that suffering helps nothing, they no longer want to suffer or do anything at all. But we must do good works and suffer, not so that we thereby abolish our sins before God, but because flesh and blood do not want to be righteous and thus must be mortified. One must put a leash around its neck that it not be too lecherous. If the monks heard and believed this they would say, "What am I still doing in the monastery?" The Scripture pulls external righteousness down to earth. It does not eliminate sin but leads one into a chaste, honorable life in the flesh. All of our suffering is not sufficient to abolish one single, forgivable sin. Look out when you read about the example of the saints and hear preaching about their patience, that you do not allow yourself to be seduced and mix your suffering and Christ's suffering together! Your suffering is an earthly suffering and a work to mortify your flesh. Christ's suffering is a heavenly suffering and a work that makes you righteous.

Therefore whoever becomes a monk, dons a cowl and tortures himself, condemns the suffering of Christ and retains nothing of it because he seeks through his own suffering what is obtained for us through Christ's suffering alone. It is not written that you should bear your sins, but: "Here is the Lamb of God, who takes away the sin of the world!" (John 1:29), and "Surely he has borne our infirmities and carried our diseases" (Isaiah 53:4).

Indeed this error is so deeply engrained in us that a strong exhortation is necessary. Our suffering has a great appearance and receives more praise than Christ's suffering. But say: Suffering here! Suffering there! But it is written: "Here is the Lamb of God!" There lies the sin of the world. If it is a matter of putting away and paying for sins, then despise your suffering! Therefore all slogans about our suffering must have as their goal to do no damage to Christ's suffering of which the Scripture says: "Here is the Lamb of God who takes away the sin of the world!" (John 1:29) and "Upon him was the punishment that made us whole, and by his bruises we are healed... The Lord has laid on him the iniquity of us all" (Isaiah 53:5, 6).

For this reason Christ's Passion must therefore be preached so that each person considers it true for him or herself. If you look at Christ hanging on the cross with his wounds, then consider: These are my sins! and do not think about your suffering!

But is it not a great pity that throughout the world they prattle on and on about Christ for many hours and thus they have the words about which we are preaching in their mouths, and yet no one preaches, understands, or pays attention to what the words mean? Otherwise they would not be against us and would not persecute us. To be sure they sing, write, and preach these words, and play them on the organ, but no one understands them. For this is their opinion: Christ has done his part, now it is necessary that we also do ours. So the power is taken from Christ's suffering and given to our suffering. This is of the devil.

However, no one believes what a dangerous thing it is to preach our suffering with the added assumption that it abolishes sins. Conversely, it is by far the greatest thing to preach Christ's suffering in such a way that we may take our stand on it. These godless people have written their Passion books[1] and said: Whoever meditates on the Passion in a cursory manner earns the forgiveness of sins. Thus they have made a work of my contemplation and imagine: that does it! For this reason learn the Passion well and distinguish rightly Christ's suffering and our suffering and patience.

To be sure, Paul says, "I am now rejoicing in my suffering for your sake, and in my flesh I am completing what is lacking in Christ's afflictions for the sake of his body, that is, the church" (Col. 1:24). Your suffering serves to improve things on earth and to spread the Gospel more and more. But take Christ's suffering and lay all your sins on him. Therefore Christ's suffering was preached from the beginning of the world, and the dear Patriarchs have, from the beginning of the world, insisted that the suffering which redeems from sin may be attributed to no one but to this Man. So you say: I will gladly suffer and be patient, but by this I will not abolish one single pardonable sin. Rather it is written that Christ's suffering takes away sin. Christ's suffering alone truly swallows up sin and death. You must give the honor to him. Faith does not cling to our suffering. If it did, it would be idolatry. You must grasp Christ's suffering by faith alone.

In conclusion: Do not mix your suffering with Christ's suffering, but separate them from one another like heaven from earth, or gold from manure. If our opponents regarded it this way, they would not be our enemy. In the entire year Christ is not so tortured as at this season, when he is shamefully spit upon and blasphemed—just as he was on the cross. This teaching cannot be drummed in enough. For it pains Satan grievously, and the flesh always wants us to erect trust in our suffering. Let this be said as a warning. This text and the one in Isaiah [53:4] let you be certain: "Here is the Lamb of God who takes away the sin of the world" (John 1:29).

"When they had sung the hymn" [Mark 14:26]. There you see how the disciples are an example for us, since they, too, relied on their works and were angry with Christ. Because Christ became weak, they think they have to help and assist the weak Lord, and they are easily angered at him. This arrogance is implanted in us all by nature. Peter wants to die with him; another wants to be arrested with him. That is, we would like to let what we do amount to something. But this is the greatest article of faith, to believe that no one should nor can take away our sins but Christ alone. On the other hand, our human nature says: If you have sinned, then do penance, do this and do that! And yet it should not be; we should know no other penance than Christ's suffering. Indeed we grasp this through no monk's cowl, but through this Word alone: "Here is the Lamb of God who takes away the sin of the world" (John 1:29).

In this way, the disciples stumbled. This reflects the fact that in the world there can be nothing but denials and no other sermon than that Christ be denied. For to preach that we become pure by our own works is a denial of Christ. Of course we would gladly give our bodies for ourselves. But instead we must remain in Christ's body which is given for us.

"Gethsemane" [Mark 14:32]. Christ admonishes his disciples and us all to pray that we do not fall into temptation. Yes indeed, I have said this to you often and continue to say: Be thankful that you are given the Gospel and take care that you stick with it. You see the terrifying case. The Enthusiasts, who praise nothing but the Spirit, have fallen away from this. They have this sermon of Christ alone in their mouths but do not understand it. Instead each one grabs for his or her own works. The Anabaptists sell their goods and go about in plain clothes. But whoever wants to be a Christian dare not be blind to the fact that we need not behave this way. Let everyone remain in their own clothes! Sour looks and plain garments do not a Christian make! Such people have fallen away from the Gospel because they have not prayed.

Christ says, "Pray" [Luke 22:40]. Satan does not rest but prowls around to scatter you, desiring to "sift all of you like wheat" (Luke 22:31). When one sifts, the sieve goes around so that no grain remains unmoved. This is what the devil does to Christians so that they lose the Gospel and do not know what they are to believe, as happened to Peter. Let us take the example of the apostles and be diligent in prayer. I am concerned that after our time shameful preachers will come who will torment you indeed more than we do. Already we suffer persecution because we preach Christ.

"Keep awake and pray, for the spirit indeed is willing, but the flesh is weak" [Mark 14:38]. The dear disciples are sad that he wants to go away, and they do not want to be separated from him. This sadness results in their becoming weary and falling asleep in prayer. For this reason Christ says, "Keep awake and pray, for the spirit indeed is willing, but the flesh is weak." There is disagreement whether this is said of Christ or of the apostles.[2] I believe he says it of both. Our flesh is sinful. This is Christ's customary way of speaking (cf. Matt. 16:17; John 3:6, 6:63). Even Paul says, "For what the flesh desires is opposed to the Spirit" (Gal. 5:17). I would like to be righteous, but the flesh is opposed.

"My Father, if it is possible, let this cup pass from me" [Matthew 26:39]. This weakness in Christ's flesh is an example meant to comfort us when we also become weak, so that we not despair and do not reject others who are weak. For our sake Christ has become weak. Our sins, not his, lie around his neck. If they lie on our conscience, that's the wrong place for them; they should lie in the flesh, but not in the conscience. That is, we should discipline the flesh and restrain it. But in the conscience a person should be free and neither bother oneself about sins nor be concerned to abolish them. Although Christ is weak according to the flesh, yet his spirit is vigorous and will destroy sin. If you see Christ suffer, cry out and lament, then think: It is your sin. But this is by far the hardest thing of all; it doesn't fit our expectations. How can reason believe it?

"So Judas brought a detachment of soldiers together with police from the chief priests and the Pharisees. . . ." [John 18:3ff.]. There you can see that Jesus must come to his suffering at the hands of his own disciple who betrays him with a kiss. With this Judas gives them a sign as if to say: It will be dark in the garden, and if they hear us coming, one will flee this way and another that way. In order that you do not seize a disciple, watch me! And therefore he is concerned that Christ does not escape, having completely forgotten about his miracles. For this reason he says: watch me and give me a light!

In this story we comprehend what happens to Christ and the Gospel in this world. This is Christ's greatest suffering: that his disciples are scattered and Judas betrays him. And he laments as in the Psalm: "Even my bosom friend, in whom I trusted, who ate of my bread has lifted the heel against me" (Psalm 41:9). Now it does not yet appear that it hurts Christ, but in our experience we feel it. Those who are with us in the Gospel are our betrayers. For if Müntzer and other devils had not made mistakes concerning rebellion and the Sacrament, the papacy would be weak as a fly.[3]

It seems that Judas kissed the Lord like a real rogue. For he probably thought: If I come and offer him a kiss, he will not expect that I am about to betray him but will consider it an offer of friendship. Then they will sneak up on him and take him prisoner. This is a great and devilish wickedness that he betrays the Lord with a kiss, and yet he does not want to be called a betrayer because he uses the sign of friendship. And the Lord receives him as a friend: You are my friend, if only you wanted to be! Understand that it was the custom in that land that those who greeted one another kissed. Such was the custom there and so Christ also greets his disciples. They were a courteous people. But the finer the gesture, the more poisonous the people.

This is one part of the Passion story. His suffering begins in the garden. Because our sin began in the garden, the Passion also begins in the garden.[4]

"First they took him to Annas, who was the father-in-law of Caiaphas" (John 18:13). Caiaphas had married the daughter of Annas. They had wanted to flatter the old high priest, so they delivered to him as the elder the evildoer whom they had taken prisoner. Then Annas ran over to the house of Caiaphas, and there all the priests gathered. There Peter also denied the Lord three times. If

Christ had not prayed for him, his faith would have come to an end and he would have despaired.

Take careful notice of Christ's stripes and wounds for they are our sins. And read inscribed on the bonds, chains, and blows: mine, mine, my sins! so that we preserve ourselves from boasting in our own suffering, as when one boasts that humility and patience are the highest virtues, as if they brought about the forgiveness of sins. But forgiveness of sin is all written in the suffering, patience, and humility of this Man. This we should learn well! For human nature is of a different opinion, and what the pope and the fathers praise and preach teaches something else.

Endnotes

[1] Passion books were picture books of Christ's suffering. During his lifetime Albrecht Dürer alone produced four such books. See *Albrecht Dürer 1471 bis 1528: Das gesamte graphische Werk,* introduced by Wolfgang Hütt, 2 vols. (Herrsching, Germany: Manfred Pawlak, 1982), 2:1483–87, 1522–47, 1590–1629, 1848–63.

[2] Luther seems to be referring to a debate among various interpreters on this text, although no discussion occurs in Nicholas of Lyra's commentary or in the *Ordinary Gloss.*

[3] Luther was of the opinion that the Peasants' Revolt and the Lord's Supper controversy had prevented the spread of the Gospel and thus protected the papacy. See Mark U. Edwards, *Luther and the False Brethren* (Stanford: Stanford University Press, 1975).

[4] This connection was made throughout the Middle Ages, for example in the *Ordinary Gloss* on John 18:1.

Good Friday Afternoon
March 26, 1529
The Passion: Trial and Crucifixion

There is much in this text, but the time is short. For this reason we want to deal with it simply for the children and tell the story.

Peter went out and wept bitterly for having betrayed the Lord. However, the chief priests and the elders sought false testimony against the Lord in order to put him to death, but they found none. The text says, "They were looking for a false testimony" [Matthew 26:59]. But they could come up with no uniform testimony. It costs a hundred times more to establish a lie than to tell the truth. There stand the all-powerful and all-knowing lords, and they are unable to find a few false testimonies. Thus we may see how powerless the lie is against the truth, that Satan with all his members cannot produce one pretext, not even a hair's breadth wide that has the appearance of a pretext. There Satan is splendidly defied. Indeed many false witnesses came, one heard it this way, another that way.

"At last two false witnesses came forward" [Matthew 26:60]. But even they did not agree. One said one thing, the other something else. The one said, "This fellow has said, 'I am able to destroy the temple of God and to build it in three days'" [Matthew 26:61]. But Jesus did not say with his hands! The other said, "He has said, 'Destroy this temple, and in three days I will raise it up'" (John 2:19). Now because the witnesses did not corroborate one another, which is what everyone wanted, the chief priest says to Jesus, "Have you no answer? What is it that they testify against you?" [Matthew 26:62]. An open lie is not worthy of an answer but gives its own answer. For this reason the Lord is silent. He knows full well that they themselves realize their charges are nothing.

Then the high priest said: "I put you under oath before the living God, are you the Messiah, the Son of the Blessed One?" [Matthew 26:63, Mark 14:61]. Godless people give the Lord high enough names. So even today the Jews do this. When they want to indicate something in the Scripture, they do not say, "Thus says God or Christ," but much higher and holier: "This is what the Holy One and the Highly Praised One says!" that one should think they honor him more than all the people on earth. Therefore even our hypocrites say: "Jesus our Savior." When the Turks draw into battle, they all yell "God, God, God!" Therefore all desperate betrayers and evildoers appear as if they were holier than others, even though they are the most wretched. This Caiaphas also did here.

But Jesus answers: "You have said so. But I tell you, from now on you will see the Son of Man seated at the right hand of Power and coming on the clouds of heaven" [Matthew 26:64]. Then they were certain of the matter, since he calls himself Son of God and says he will sit at the right hand of Power and will come again. There they surely have him; he has blasphemed God and is worthy of death. For this reason all the other priests said, "He deserves death" [Matthew 26:66].

"Then they spat in his face and struck him; and some slapped him, saying, 'Prophesy to us, you Messiah! Who is it that struck you?'" [Matthew 26:67f.]. Many have written in Passion booklets[1] that much disgrace and shame befell Christ on this night that would not be revealed before the Last Day. This I pass over. I do not reject such devotions. But I would like one to draw the conclusions that need to be drawn. You better believe that it happened in the presence of the chief priests. The servants saw that their masters condemned him as the greatest evildoer because he said, "You will see the Son of Man seated at the right hand of power and coming on the clouds of heaven" [Matthew 26:64]. Reason said at once: "Shame! Should one tolerated this evildoer?" For this reason the servants approached and wanted to flatter their masters with pleasantries: the one pulled his hair and another spit on him. Thus it goes even today with the Gospel.

"When morning came, all the chief priests and the elders of the people conferred together against Jesus in order to bring about his death" [Matthew 27:1]. Whether he was questioned twice or only once is uncertain.[2] A few say he was questioned for the first time during the night in the house of Caiaphas; the second time in the morning when the other high priests came and Christ was asked again whether he confesses that he is the Christ. Be it once or twice, about this I do not quarrel. But what concerns me most of all is that we consider the suffering of the Lord as that which he suffers for us. People preach little about this and think about it even less. The blows, the spit, the slander: these are all our sins, and every Christian should regard it as if this was written over it: My sin! For on this day one should preach that our sins lie on the neck of the Lord so that we might know where our sin lies and where it should lie.

Now after they had interrogated the Lord and had established the charge: "He has blasphemed!" [Matthew 26:65], they imagined that they had quite certainly found the grounds for his death. And they did not consider that it would not be necessary to take this before Pilate. Before Pilate they would have to speak differently, namely, "If you release this man, you are no friend of the emperor" (John 19:12).

"When Judas, his betrayer, saw that Jesus was condemned, he repented and brought back the thirty pieces of silver to the chief priests and elders. He said, 'I have sinned by betraying innocent blood.' But they said, 'What is that to us? See to it yourself'"

[Matthew 27:3-4]. To such a penitent belongs such a confessor. Indeed Judas confessed his sins, but to one who had no authority to absolve him. Instead he came to those who committed a still greater sin. Judas would have been saved if he had had a true, evangelical confessor.

Why had he not earlier considered that he was betraying innocent blood at the time when he kissed the Lord? When his last hour and the remorse arrive and there is no preacher or confessor present, then it happened. Everyone who is hardened should take this example to heart, so that they see how the devil rewards his servants. Judas betrayed the Lord for thirty pieces of silver! As soon as Judas served the devil, he gave him a reward. Judas is an example and picture of all who serve the devil. The devil made him despair, so that he threw away the money and hung himself in shame before all the Jews.

They said to him, "What is that to us? See to it yourself" (Matthew 27:4). At this point nobody said, You have not done evil, but you have served the chief priests and obeyed the authorities. Instead they ask, "What is that to us?" The Scripture says of those who remain alone and have no comforter, "Woe to the one who is alone and falls and does not have another to help" (Eccles. 4:10). A monk is one such person who lives alone separated from people. A monastery is actually a devil's tavern. For God has not created people to be alone, but God has determined that a person should serve others. Judas was also a monk: If somebody had been with him, then he would not have despaired. Therefore someone once said, "A person who likes to be alone is either God or a beast, either a devil or an angel." For the human being is, as the philosophers have handed down, a social creature who should serve others and love them.[3]

But if this is so, then such a creature must have companionship. To counter this the devil has made living alone so glorious with the saying, "You who want to live apart will always keep the purest heart." I think they remain pure when they are outside the monastery, even if they soil themselves on occasion; but inside, one becomes a whoremonger. Judas is the father of monks. He hung himself on a tree and his belly burst. The devil had his own way with him.

"But the chief priests, taking the pieces of silver, said, 'It is not lawful to put them into the treasury, since they are blood money'" [Matthew 27:6]. The holy people hit the mark. They did this after the ascension of the Lord. There they are: executing the Lord and yet

Maundy Thursday Afternoon
March 25, 1529
The Passion: Anointing in Bethany, Last Supper, and Footwashing

We have proposed to preach on the Passion of Christ over three days and not, as was done in the past, for eight hours straight. Instead we want to divide it up over five hours. We do this so that the Passion story might continue to be known among the laity. I will simply read the text condensed from the four gospels,[1] because for the rest of the year, you hear sermons on Wednesdays and Saturdays devoted to the two Evangelists (Matthew and John), where all of these texts are interpreted at a slower pace. For this reason, this is to be a simple sermon, in which we will read the text.

This morning I admonished you that on account of God's command and promise and our need, we should not despise the Sacrament. I urge not only you older folks, but also the young, to cling to the 10 Commandments, the Creed, and the Lord's Prayer. This has already happened with us older folks. Now the children must be instructed and recite before the deacons what they have learned at were not friends with each other, but now they are all the best of friends. Had the Gospel not come, the Franciscans, too, would have devoured themselves.

Pilate was a clever man, so he proposes Barabbas. For he knew that they must regard him as a murderer, and he thought: Long before they want Barabbas freed, they will let three Jesuses go. For this reason he used reasonable prudence and placed before them Jesus and Barrabas.

Then Pilate passed sentence: "I will therefore have him flogged and release him" [Luke 23:16]. He reasoned in this way: I will banish him from the city; that will satisfy them. Now everyone had to assemble, even the soldiers, who did more than Pilate commanded and crowned him. All peoples sin against him. Concerning this the Evangelists go into great detail. Where it is a matter of mockery they use many words, but they describe the crucifixion in the briefest fashion: "When they came to the place that is called The Skull, they crucified Jesus" [Luke 23:33]. They have seen so much shame that it pains them deeply. If we were to interpret everything in detail we would have to preach three, four, five years on it.

Myrrh, vinegar, gall mixed together is a fine drink for a languishing person (Mark 15:23; Matthew 27:34)!

Now Christ is crucified and hangs on the tree where he is a priest. Here everyone has to pay attention to the words: "Father, forgive them; for they do not know what they are doing" [Luke 23:34]. Each one should look at Christ as he hangs on the cross as the true High Priest and pope. For this belongs to the High Priest according to the Old Testament, that he be adorned and decked out with fine garments and make a sacrifice. Therefore here Christ exercises his priestly office. How? He has on his best garments and adornment. Which? Patience and obedience to the Father. You have never seen greater love, humility and gentleness. Here every possible virtue comes together. Clothed in these robes, he sacrifices not calves' blood, but his own blood. And he does it for us and prays, "Father, forgive them for they do not know what they are doing!"

This is the text which commands us to acknowledge Christ as our true High Priest. There would be much to preach and to pursue. Christ prays for those who have nailed him to the cross and especially for those who do not know what they did. Some make a distinction that he prays for those who do not know it but not for those who do know it, who have committed the sin against the Holy Spirit.⁶ But of this we will not speak now. If this prayer does not extend to us, our cowls and tonsures won't help. The prayer of this High Priest must help.

Endnotes

¹A popular form of medieval religious literature, heavily illustrated and focused on Christ's suffering and anguish.

²For Luther's freedom in interpretation, see Heinrich Bornkamm, *Luther and the Old Testament,* trans. Eric W. and Ruth C. Gritsch, ed. Victor I. Gruhn (Philadelphia: Fortress Press, 1969), 188–95.

³Aristotle, *Politics* I.2

⁴Luther translates Luke 23:11 "in a white robe" and not, as in the NRSV, "an elegant robe."

⁵John Cochlaeus. See p.44, note 7.

⁶The commentary of Nicholas of Lyra (c. 1270–1340) on Luke 23:34 suggested this interpretation.

Holy Saturday Morning
March 27, 1529
The Passion: Words from the Cross

"Father, forgive them; for they do not know what they are doing" (Luke 23:34). Yesterday you heard about the prayer which the Lord prayed as High Priest for those who nailed him on the cross. I could say a lot about this, but we must move on. We must pay attention to this prayer, because it concerns us. All our life, all our prayer, both good and evil, is comprehended in this prayer. And this is the prayer that the letter to the Hebrews describes when it says, "In the days of his flesh, Jesus offered up prayers and supplications, with loud cries and tears, to the one who was able to save him from death, and he was heard because of his reverent submission" (Hebrews 5:7). This prayer has taken away the power of the devil and opened up heaven and every grace.

Yesterday I told you to make a distinction between Christ and all the saints, so that we are not found among the hypocrites, who with their works and prayers seek salvation—just as the Turks think they need no mediator. We must be found among the multitude for whom Christ prays: "Father, forgive them; for they do not know what they are doing!" Make a distinction among prayers as among works and suffering! Our prayers are nothing and are not heard unless they share in this prayer and are written under the little word "Forgive them!" I must count myself among the number of sinners for whom Christ prayed here. Now you may also say: Whatever I may pray, that is enough! But I say this not without reason, for the devil never rests. To be sure we must admonish the people at all times to do good. However, it is ten times more necessary to keep the chief Christian teaching. If this is carried through, then the works will most certainly follow. For this reason our comfort is that we share in this prayer and that Christ prays for us.

There are two kinds of sinners. The first are the evildoers, who do not believe, and the arrogant saints. The second are those who believe in forgiveness through Christ. We are indeed sinners but under the shadow of Christ's merit and prayer, which he has performed as our High Priest. Consider this word well and do not skip over it, namely, that the prayer spoken over you with tears was prayed by a true High Priest and is heard by God. For this reason no one is excluded from this prayer except those who are unbelievers or arrogant saints. Other preachers make only an example from this prayer as they did with Christ's suffering.

"Pilate also had an inscription written and put on the cross. It read, 'Jesus of Nazareth, the King of the Jews'" [John 19:19]. Much has been written about this inscription as that by which the people should cross themselves in the morning. The words are good as long as one believes them and does not make an idol out of them. This inscription was nailed to the cross in order to shame Christ so that it might appear he was a rebel. But now the title has become so great an honor that there is nothing holier or purer than this title. Whoever is not under this inscription is condemned.

"The King of the Jews." Christ was falsely accused as if he were an earthly king. But the guilt and the lies have been transformed into innocence and truth, and what those people laughed about we take seriously. So it is with everything in the Gospel. "To one a fragrance from death to death," but to us sinners "a fragrance from life to life" [2 Cor. 2:16]. Even today Christ is thought to be a rebel, but among us he is the King of glory. Among the papacy our Gospel is poison and lies, but among us it is light. Therefore a Christian should also gladly receive the title of rebel. But only if we are "Jews,"[1] that is, those who confess and give thanks and praise, who confess all good things come from God. For when we praise Christ, his works, his righteousness and strength and make ourselves into nothing, we are true "Jews." Among these people, who do not justify themselves with their own works, he is the true king.

"When the soldiers had crucified Jesus, they took his clothes" [John 19:23]. I also preached on this previously in John's gospel.[2] There John makes much of the text concerning the clothes for which the soldiers divided and cast lots, although this clearly happened only after Christ's death. But John indicates a spiritual interpretation. It is written as a part of the story so that we may see how single-mindedly the people who crucified Christ behaved. Thus they rob him of his clothes as if he were a criminal.

In our day, the Enthusiasts,[3] who write against us with great certainty, have such an oversized presumption. This concerns the difficult matter of how they speak of the Last Judgment with such defiance and certainty that they curse and defy it. A Christian is full of fear and struggle and does not arrive at such security. But they remain hard as a rock and do not care that one day they could suffer for their statements, but think it will all be forgotten. This accords with the story. We believe in Christ, but sometimes he leaves us so alone as if there were no God who accepts us, and we appear so forsaken that they make a mockery and a game from it. This grieves Christians when they see in themselves such struggle and fear, but on the other side such strengths. It's always the same! Those soldiers are the fathers of all secure people.

"When Jesus saw his mother," etc. [John 19:26]. He wants to bless the world completely and depart from it. He has nothing, neither clothes nor any place to lay his head nor even a place on earth a foot wide where he may die nor a bed on which to lie. Instead he hangs in midair. But he still has his mother and the disciple. At this point he gives his mother away to his dearest disciple whom he loves. This is a great pain when he has to depart from them and can no longer take care of his mother and the disciple. See how otherwise disposed are the dying when they must leave their loved ones. Christ must not cling to the goods of the world.

From this text we have made an idol of Mary. When Christ and his suffering were preached, at the same time they also preached about his mother. The papists said, Mary is given to us as our mother, so we must take refuge in her. We want to regard Mary with all the honor of which she is worthy, but we do not want to make her the same as her Son. She has not died for us and has not prayed for us. Honor her as you want, but you should not honor her as you honor Christ. For this reason the Lord also sends her away and wants to be alone, so that we cling to him. But we do the opposite: we send the Son away and cling to his mother. Christ forsakes the earth so that he may be able to help us. But we want his mother to intercede for us! John took in Jesus' mother as his own mother. She took care of and attended to his home and had a place where she could remain as a widow who had lost her son. She is truly our mother, but to build our faith on her takes from Christ his suffering, honor, and office.

"Those who passed by derided him, shaking their heads and saying, 'Aha! You who would destroy the temple and build it in three days'" [Mark 15:29]. This is now an example or work. The dear holy Evangelists emphasize strongly the mockery and make a greater suffering out of it than out of the physical torture. Here they describe every humiliation by the chief priests and scribes, the soldiers and the thief on the cross. As the saying goes, "The laugh is always on the losers."[4] It wasn't enough that they stripped him. No one mocks the thieves; they are given good wine! But the one between the thieves must suffer. There can be no one on earth as wicked as Christ; he must be the most evil. No one looks at the thieves on the cross. All eyes and poisonous arrows are aimed at Christ. The devil forgets all the others, so envious and violent is he towards Christ. That is why Satan took revenge against him in this way. For this reason he takes even his clothes and lets them be gambled for. The devil is by far and away the most shameful. He takes his life, finally his mother. He did all he could; he omitted nothing.

I will say nothing of the torment of Christ's soul, about which we do not know and also will never experience. For he suffered not only in body but also in soul and heart. Satan has cooled down now because he poured out all his wrath and wickedness on Christ. For this reason Satan is now weak with those who trust in Christ, so that he is thrust out with a single word. When he hears "Jesus Christ" spoken in true faith or simply "Jesus of Nazareth," Satan falls as if thunderstruck. He has burnt himself out, he has poured out all his poison, so that he has become quite powerless. But only for those who believe. For others he is the Prince of the World. Everything that Jesus has done—dying in great torment, agony, shame and poverty—was done for this purpose.

Now follows an example to confirm his teaching about "Father, forgive them!" It is an example to us of the thief who rebukes his brother: "Do you not fear God, since you are under the same sentence of condemnation?" [Luke 23:40]. As if he were to say: Are you simply going to follow the crowd? Are you crazy and foolish? Don't you see that you must die? Others in your predicament might have ceased their wicked deeds, but you still do such evil in the face of death! This is one fine, sharp rebuke coming right from the spirit: "We are getting what we deserve for our deeds" [Luke 23:41].

Look at what the Gospel is doing here! Where those around him are silent, then the stones (Luke 19:40) and the thief must confess Christ. In the entire Bible I have found no example that is more filled with comfort than this verse: "Jesus, remember me when you come into your kingdom" [Luke 23:41]. There he hangs in his pain, where he should have despaired, and yet he becomes a preacher and preaches the whole of Moses to his brother and speaks openly against the priests and scribes who had opened wide their traps and regarded Christ as nothing. This thief had so strong a heart that he does not consider this at all. "This man has done nothing wrong" [Luke 23:42]. What faith! Since all judge Christ to be guilty, only this man stands against them all. This is like a judge's verdict. He condemns all enemies of Christ and the offense of the cross; he does not look at all on the humiliation but instead appeals to Christ alone as his mediator. Pilate and all the rest do Christ an injustice. "This man has done nothing wrong."

These are simple words, but the heart of the thief is greater than heaven and earth. Even in the midst of this gruesome affair he could confess the Christian faith! Is this not a terrible scandal that Christ dies and they all mock him? And yet because of such humiliation, Christ does not climb down from the cross as he should have. Indeed the thief does not look at such scandal but looks at and appeals to Christ alone. He must have had pure eyes. For he does not see what is weak in Christ but he sees what does not appear, namely, that he is a king and has a kingdom in which to live.

This is the first fruit of Christ's prayer, "Father, forgive them; for they do not know what they are doing!" The prayer concerns his brother who is crucified with him. Luke speaks of both thieves. Some understand this as synecdoche,[5] that is, an abbreviated way of speaking. To each his own. This thief certainly had not previously recognized the Lord as the Christ. But as the Lord prayed, he recognized him and perceived the sheer hatred and envy of Christ's enemies and that they had no grounds for condemning him. And finally the light came and broke through so that it occurred to him: He is a righteous man! Would to God that I was where he is. Then came the recognition that he was a king. And Christ answered him: "Truly I tell you, today you will be with me in Paradise!" [Luke 23:43].

This is a powerful word. For this reason we want to celebrate the thief: let his story be the first and best in Christianity! Here you have described how a person becomes a Christian. The monks are ashamed to be like this thief.[6] But don't you be ashamed to be a Christian according to the example of the thief. But you say, "I am indeed no murderer!" Yes you are! As long as you are under the devil who is a murderer (John 8:44). This thief is the first saint in the New Testament and became such through the suffering of Christ who prayed for him on the cross. Therefore we all become Christians just as he did. Would to God that we knew it! But it is an example that is not as easy to follow as it is to look at. The thief is an abbot who is worth more than any Bernard or Benedict. No one has done what he did, and no one, including all the monks, will ever do it. For what is monkery in comparison to him? First, we are all sinners. The thief pronounces the judgment on himself that he is a sinner. But the monks never do such things. But those who want to come to Christ must first confess their sins, feel and believe them. Moreover, this is an art that supersedes all others, one to which I cannot attain, because the torment struck him right along side the sin so that he knew immediately what he should have done.

If I say, "I am a sinner" and am in no danger of punishment, this is quite easy. But if the punishment of sin is added to the sin, then to recognize it as just and to consent to it is an art that no monk or cleric can perform. The thief accepts the punishment he feels and says yes to it and bears it willingly and gladly as if he were saying: Indeed it happens to me justly and I gladly suffer it. Whoever can do this has already conquered but whoever cannot stands in great danger.

Therefore this is the art to be learned by all Christians, to know they are sinners whose flesh is full of sins. Likewise it is an art if wrath and terror come before death, if having been thrown into that prison, they say: This is just. When that does not happen, there is no guarantee that we will be saved. The thief said, I am a sinner, it is fair that I be punished. But then what does he do? He turns to Christ. Those who live their holy lives do not come to the point that they call their works sin. They are in a different order from that of the thief. But they want their actions to be right and refuse to learn the art the thief has mastered. Much less can they master the other art to say, when persecution comes, You are right, O Lord. Instead they say: I am being persecuted because I am a priest or monk.

This is the first work to be a Christian: to know that we are sinners and that we deserve what befalls us. So then, the thief does nothing other than to believe and call on Christ. There is no fasting or making pilgrimages. He casts his eyes on him: "Lord, remember me when you come into your kingdom!" These are words of faith. He confesses that Christ is a king and has a kingdom, and he cries out, "Lord, remember me!" This is everything: first, to accuse oneself and second, to make no claim to be righteous, but instead to turn to Christ. This is the Gospel, that one does not become a Christian through one's works but through Christ. This is so fine a faith that it is a joy. He is so certain that he does not waver an inch. He is put here as an example.

But now someone will say: The thief was a special case. Not everyone experiences this! But either you must go by this standard or by none at all. Christ's prayer must precede, you must acknowledge that you are a sinner and that everything bad which happens to you happens fairly, and finally you must fix your eyes on him. Then the fifth thing will also follow: "Today you will be with me in Paradise." There he immediately has the promise without penance or merit, and Paradise is given to him because he is a "Jew," that is, he confesses rightly. Then the title comes into play: "King of the Jews."[7] The thief shares in his kingdom. Set that example against all presumption and against all despair and regard the thief as an example, not just a miracle, although it is that, too. Thus with all his sins he clings only to

Christ, freely confessing them and clinging to grace alone. This is difficult for human nature. The thief made this confession to the entire world as an example full of comfort.

Endnotes

[1] Luther follows the etymology of the word "Jew" in Jerome's *De nominibus Hebraicis* (PL 23:781).

[2] This sermon is preserved in WA 28:392f. Luther preached on this text the previous Saturday, 20 March 1529, as part of the weekly sermons based on a continuous reading of the fourth gospel.

[3] See above, p. 62 note 3.

[4] This saying is no. 245 in Ernst Thiele, *Luthers Sprichwörtersammlung* (Weimar: Böhlau, 1900). Literally: "Whoever suffers injury cannot worry about insult."

[5] A figure of speech where the whole is taken for the part or the part for the whole. Noting that in Matthew 27:44 both thieves mock Jesus, the *Ordinary Gloss* and Nicholas of Lyra explain it this way. The *Interlinear Gloss*, citing Jerome, gives Luther's explanation.

[6] Here Luther contrasts medieval expectations of progress in the Christian life to his understanding of the Gospel.

[7] See above, note 1.

Holy Saturday Afternoon
March 27, 1529
The Passion: Words from the Cross
Death and Burial

We will deal with the text in its entirety and conclude the Passion. "And from noon on, darkness came over the whole land until three in the afternoon" [Matthew 27:45]. This was a great sign, so it is hardly surprising that all would be so upset. Such darkness lasted from the sixth to the ninth hour. The astronomers know well enough what kind of darkness this is.[1] The sixth hour according to the Hebrew numbering is the twelfth hour according to the German way. They have divided the day into four parts: from the sixth to the ninth, from the ninth to the twelfth, from the twelfth to the third, and from the third to the sixth. From the sixth hour to the ninth hour Christ was judged; from the ninth to the twelfth hour he was crucified. Then a great darkness covered the entire land.

It was a great miracle. For thus science tells us: If there is a full moon then it is impossible that there be an eclipse. Yet here it happens in the middle of the day or soon after midday at the time of a full moon. If the sun is darkened it must happen in the new moon. They, however, were obliged to celebrate the Passover at the full moon. For this reason that was a sign which they could not tolerate.

"And about three o'clock Jesus cried out with a loud voice, 'Eli, Eli lama sabachthani?'" [Matthew 27:46].[2] The evangelists wrote this verse in Hebrew in order to indicate that this Psalm (22) speaks of Christ. Why is it that one quarrels so much over this verse? We still don't understand that the one who is to be our Savior cries out that he is forsaken. It is the Lord who takes away our sins and these sins separate us from God, from righteousness and from every good. He had to taste this separation on the cross so that we come to realize Christ's suffering must be distinguished from all other suffering. This, however, is the best part, that he did not despair, but cried out to God. What it means to be forsaken by God I cannot say enough about, and even if I could, you would still not understand it all. They took body and life from him and humiliated him so that no one confessed him, except the thief.

Now these last words, which he spoke at the point of death, also fall victim to insults. No more poisonous hatred or envy has ever been heard than that which Christ suffered on the cross. They cannot even regard his words in a good light. "When some of the bystanders heard it, they said, 'This man is calling for Elijah'" [Matthew 27:47]. They may well have understood it and simply perverted it out of rank malice. Some interpreters say that the soldiers mocked his words because they did not understand the language.[3] But it is more likely that the Jews mocked him in this most scornful way, as when a child cries, "Mother, Mother" and some evil person says, "Yes, bother, bother!"[4] This is what the devil does. In Christ's deepest need, the devil perverts his words.

There is a lot that could be preached on this text. This the devil can do, namely, that out of great hatred he belittles and scoffs at our prayers and words. The people who write against us would also like to do this, but they are too coarse. The devil, however, knows right well what is in the heart: When a person wants to appeal to God earnestly, he wrings a mockery from it. And it is not enough that they mocked the Lord with words but also with actions. Someone offered him a drink of vinegar.

"At once one of them ran and got a sponge, filled it with sour wine, put it on a stick, and gave it to him to drink" [Matthew 27:48]. They brought this out on his account, for they had offered the other thieves a drink of wine: Sure, they said, he thirsts, so give him something to drink! Here appear the hatred and envy of a thousand devils. As soon as he opened his mouth, he is mocked. When he became thirsty, they offered him a drink of vinegar. No one does this to a desperate, treacherous criminal, even if he is about to be quartered. They gave vinegar only to the one unjustly judged. If he had desired a bed, they would have pierced him with spear and nail. So it shall be: every cruelty is to befall Christ and his Gospel so that Satan may pour out absolutely every evil he possesses and become powerless, much to our comfort.

"Then Jesus, crying with a loud voice, said, 'Father into your hands I commend my spirit'" [Luke 23:46]. To cover this would take a separate sermon on how one should die.[5]

"Now when Jesus had received the wine, he said, 'It is finished.' Then he bowed his head and gave up his spirit" [John 19:30]. The Scripture is fulfilled, for it is written that the Lamb of God must die for us. He is our high priest, Aaron, for on the cross he fully gives his life and sacrifices himself. Therefore it is already fulfilled. Here no one may object that there is still so much more that needs to happen.

This is the suffering that purchased our redemption. Here it is necessary to urge us not to forget this suffering so easily and be so ungrateful. For this suffering indicates what horrible thing an evil life involves. We want to be Christians and yet we live high on the hog, as if Christ had suffered for nothing or at least not for our sins. Because he died for the sake of our sins, he certainly wants sins to be put to death, and we who want to be Christians should guard ourselves our whole life long against sins, because the payment for sin cost so much and took the Lord so much to accomplish. Because we do not remember the suffering that took place for us, we do not trouble ourselves much over sin.

But, as I said, this suffering must be separated from the suffering of all the saints. No Passion should be so fully in our hearts as this one, because we should realize that our sins rest in it. Our sins drowned Christ, Satan trampled him underfoot, and Christ died for us. Now Satan rules, and sin prevails, and the Jews are happy, singing, and jumping: There lies Christ fully in the dust. All his miracles and teaching are lost; there is no more Christ.

"At that moment the curtain of the temple was torn in two, from top to bottom" [Matthew 27:51]. Soon it begins. Now that the suffering is over, things are quickly reversed, death must have a sendoff, because it is to be defeated. The dead rise[6] but Christ still remains in death. Because they want to bury him, others rise up. All creatures are aroused when the Passion is accomplished, as if they wanted to say, "It must be another!" Those who see these things must have iron hearts. The sun loses its brilliance, the rocks split, the earth shakes, which is a frightening thing. And the graves of the saints are opened, and the saints who have recently died come out. I believe Simeon[7] was one of them. And the curtain in the temple is torn from top to bottom. This could by no means be an accident. It was made of the most festive and finest red silk. What does this mean? It means that through Christ everything is revealed and death must get out. That is, Christ indicated, even before he arose, that he could raise the dead while still lying in the grave. He did not want to rise alone but wanted to have companions who would rise and crawl out from the earth.

"Now when the centurion and those with him, who were keeping watch over Jesus, saw the earthquake and what took place, they were terrified and said, 'Truly this man was the Son of God!'" [Matthew 27:54]. The centurion, although he is also a Gentile, also begins to scold Herod and the chief priests by saying: Upon my soul, you have done injustice to this man.

Now suppose someone were hanged and some people said: It happened to him unjustly! But this man says in addition: "This man was the Son of God" and concludes this from the miracles which took place! The unbelieving Gentile confesses Christ, although Christ's own people deny him. The one charged with seeing to the corpse dares to open his mouth! However, others, who were not so bold, beat on their breasts and said: It was done to him unjustly, but he has departed this life and will not return! But the Gentile goes away comforted. "But all his acquaintances, including the women who had followed him from Galilee, stood at a distance, watching these things" [Luke 23:49].

These women were his good friends who had come with him from Galilee, who had sold their possessions and served him, who had hoped that he would be a king, and who loved him from the heart.[8] And now just when the hope was the greatest, he ends up hanging on the gallows. They think nothing other than that he was an upright man, but that now it is all over for him.

The Evangelists write this, how lamentable it was that Christ died, how the sheep were scattered and had to hear the insults, but the Jews were happy.

"Since it was the day of Preparation, the Jews. . . .asked Pilate to have the legs of the crucified men broken and the bodies removed" [John 19:31]. Here is the sign of water and blood which flows from his side [John 19:34]. This deserves a special sermon.[9] "After these things, Joseph of Arimathea asked Pilate," etc. [John 19:38]. However much Christ is forsaken, there must still be one who holds him in honor, not only the thief, but also his follower, Joseph of Arimathea.

He was a great, wealthy citizen and yet so upright at all times that he decided not to agree with their counsel and did not want to be present when they judged Christ. Here the text lauds his behavior and says he was a secret disciple of Jesus like Nicodemus. Up to this hour he had not confessed Christ, but now he does it. But the Jews thought: Now that his master is dead, let him bury him! Isn't it amazing that someone from the council buried him, him, whom the entire council and Pilate had condemned? And, although they thought that he was gone for good, nevertheless it was a great risk to go out himself with a linen cloth and take care of the corpse. But because the Lord is dead, they let him go.

Now he is buried, "so they went with the guard and made the tomb secure by sealing the stone" [Matthew 27:66]. There sin, death, and devil are lords over Christ. Sin spared nothing on him, frightened him and completely conquered him. The world, his weak flesh, the devil, and sin have struck down righteousness and sunk the Spirit. The devil has thrust God from his throne; the devil has become God again, and hell has become heaven. But the devil who oppressed him, the flesh which conquered him, sin and death which devoured him—this is my sin, death and devil and yours. What happened to him should have happened to us. We are under sin, world and flesh, and Christ lies under them for us.

But tomorrow you will hear how Christ tramples Satan and Satan's world underfoot.

Endnotes

[1] An alternate in WA 29:248, 24 reads: "do not know."
[2] The text followed by Luther reads "Eli, Eli, lama asabthani."
[3] This interpretation is found in the *Ordinary Gloss* and Nicholas of Lyra's commentary on the text.
[4] "Mutter" and "Butter" in the German.
[5] Luther wrote such a sermon in 1519. See LW 42:97–115.
[6] See Matthew 27:52–53.
[7] See Luke 2:25–35.
[8] See Luke 8:1–3.
[9] Luther also preached on this text in connection with the weekly sermons on John. See WA 28:406ff.

Easter Sunday Morning
March 28, 1529
The Resurrection of Christ and Its Meaning

Because we have before us a glorious festival and there is much to preach about, we do not want to deal with everything at once. Instead I will first read the story for the sake of the simple folk who do not know what happened on this day, in order that they may know how it turned out.

Thus the Evangelists write: "When the sabbath was over, Mary Magdalene, and Mary the mother of James, and Salome bought spices, so that they might go and anoint him" [Mark 16:1]. The good women were sad and loved the Lord. For this reason they went out and bought spices in order to anoint the dead body in the tomb. This was a custom of the Jews to anoint the dead, as Jacob was anointed in Egypt and so, too, other kings. This was wonderfully retained among the Jews and is a praiseworthy practice. It is based upon the Scripture, which even the Patriarchs had, that the dead would rise and that after this present life there would be another. Therefore they wanted to point to the resurrection by means of this external custom.

The Evangelists write many words to indicate the exact day and hour when Christ was raised. Matthew says it happened "in the evening, as the first day of the week was dawning" [Matthew 28:1]. He reckoned that they had come to the tomb one quarter-hour before the sun rose. Matthew says it happened in the evening for the Jews, who call the entire night evening up to sunrise. As long as one does not see the sun it is evening. For this reason Matthew says it happened in the evening in which the sabbath was dawning and says it was the first day of the week.

The Jews called all days which followed the sabbath, sabbaths. They regard the true sabbath all the greater because it fell on Passover, as we speak of the first day of Easter as it is today. Therefore this happened after the great sabbath was over and another day had dawned. That is, Christ was raised on this day of Sunday. For Friday was the true Passover that began on Thursday evening. After Passover came the sabbath, when he rested and laid in the tomb, and then on the next day—Sunday—he was raised.

Now while the women went out to the grave, the following happened: "And suddenly there was a great earthquake; for an angel of the Lord, descending from the heaven came and rolled back the stone and sat on it" [Matthew 28:2]. Here it is written what happened when the Lord was raised. The guards were encamped there, and a large stone sealed the entrance so that no one could roll it away. If even one of the disciples or friends of the Lord had come, the guards were there and the entire city and Pilate would have come running out to them. By the time the angel came from heaven, the Lord had already left, for, as the text says, he was raised during the great earthquake. Only after the Lord passed through the stone with his transfigured body did the angel come down. The guards indeed heard the earthquake, but they had experienced such things before and were accustomed to them. But then the angel in white garments sat before them. This they cannot bear and do not believe, but "became like dead men" [Matthew 28:4]. People must really be hardened to endure such a jolt and afterwards take a bribe to deny it.

This is how the resurrection happened in the earthquake and alarmed the Jewish guards. The Evangelists use very few words to describe it. The angels alone proclaim it. If the earth should bring forth something great and something is about to happen, then it sets off an earthquake as is written in the psalm, "From the heavens you uttered judgment; the earth feared and was still" (Psalm 76:8).[1] Therefore when you read something great happened, an earthquake preceded it (Exodus 19:18). But that earthquake is of no concern to us, nor did it matter to the Lord but only to the guards who "became like dead men" [Matthew 28:4].

Therefore when it comes, it is a sign that the Lord will do something good. Then those who persecuted him might want to watch out, but the righteous should be comforted, because "your redemption is drawing near" (Luke 21:28). Nowadays you hear people saying about earthquakes: You wait and see what follows. The work that followed this earthquake shook the entire earth. The people became excited and wanted to jump out of their skin. Thus it is said: The Gospel causes misfortune and discord and destroys love. To be sure, when an earthquake comes there is no peace but instead cities and castles collapse. People do not stick around there if they can still flee. So, too, when the Gospel comes, one cannot think about peace.

The Gospel causes an uproar in the world, but not as if this was the Gospel's fault, but rather it's the fault of the godless people. But if they can crucify and condemn him, the heavenly Father can reawaken him during an earthquake so that they are frightened. This is how it will happen when the Last Day comes, which I hope will not long delay: the cities and castles will collapse, so that it will roar.

"Who will roll away the stone for us from the entrance to the tomb?" [Mark 16:3]. The angel, who sat on the stone and drove away the guards, has vanished. And the women are real, silly fools thinking: "Who will roll away the stone for us? What shall we do?" They are troubled and are thinking they have gone for nothing. Nevertheless their great love urges them on to the tomb. Then they become aware that the guards are gone and the stone is rolled away. Still, they can only think dark thoughts: The Jews feared that we might carry away this dead man, and for this reason they carried him away themselves.

Thus they proceeded with such heavy thoughts. "Suddenly two men in dazzling clothes stood beside them" [Luke 24:4].

They do not dare to look at the angels since they are already frightened. "But the men said to them, 'Why do you look for the living among the dead?'" [Luke 24:5]. The women went there first without the men, saw the angels, and returned to the city filled with fear. True, they saw the angels but did not listen to them; for when one is in the middle of deadly peril, it is difficult for one to hear words of life. The dear apostles and the others heard the words of the women that the tomb was open and they had seen angels. The first part they could doubtless believe. But that he lives is an idle tale to them, as Luke says, "They did not believe them" (24:11).

If one is weighed down with deep thoughts, one cannot see the truth. The apostles cannot view Christ as alive, because they have too firmly convinced themselves that he is dead and buried. Thus it is with all attacks of the devil. If someone tells you something to the contrary, it sounds like an idle tale.

Mary spoke to Peter and the other disciples, "They have taken away my Lord, and I do not know where they have laid him" (John 20:13). But although all the women said this, the disciples still did not believe it. The women, too, start to think, "It is an idle tale" and imagine that they have been deceived. For this reason, Mary Magdalene laments: "They have taken away my Lord"—the angel's words were for nothing—and she remains in this delusion.

Then "Peter and the other disciple set out" [John 20:3]. John composed these words, and John gives Peter the honor, as it ought to be and as he previously did (John 20:2), although our opponents derive from this that Peter is over John. And when they went into the tomb, they found their delusion and unbelief confirmed, as Mary Magdalene had said, "They have taken away my Lord." For Peter certainly thought that the cloths were so situated that it was not Christ who had done this, but the Jews. When he saw the linen wrappings he certainly believed that someone had carried away the Lord. Thus they sank further into unbelief. Why? They could not believe the Scripture passages about his resurrection for they did not yet know them.

"Then the disciples set out again" [John 20:10].[2] This was the second journey. The women again ran, this time with Peter and John, spoke with one another, and were perplexed only about whether the Jews or Pilate had taken the Lord away. But there was no thought of

Christ's resurrection, not even an inkling. Mary Magdalene remained in the garden when they departed again, as women are more ardent. The other women went elsewhere. Mary remained at the tomb, went in, peered and saw two angels and finally found Jesus, whom she did not recognize.

This is the one text where the Lord appears to Mary Magdalene first of all. Here the other women were not near by, as this happened in the garden by the tomb. The women went again into the city in order to announce it to the disciples, for fear had come upon them and he appeared to them all. For Christ said to them, "Go and tell my brothers" (Matthew 28:10). These are two separate appearances, to Mary Magdalene and to the other women. "While they were going, some of the guard went into the city and told the chief priests everything that had happened" [Matthew 28:11].

This is the story of Easter. Much could be preached about it, and it is worth dealing with it one part at a time.

First, what ought to follow the simple knowledge of this story, is to understand and regard the resurrection of Christ in a truly Christian fashion, because the great majority of people listen to the resurrection of Christ like a story about the Turks. To them it is a story painted on the wall. It must be something better, as we sing in the hymn, "So let our joy rise full and free; Christ our comfort true will be."[3] We must consider that it is ours, that it has to do with you and me. We should not only consider how the resurrection happened, but that you recognize that it happens for you, as the Lord says in the words: "Go and tell my brothers!" (Matthew 28:10). There we hear what he intends with his resurrection.

This is the true teaching of the resurrection: that each person receives the resurrection as his or her own. For there is a great difference between 'Christ is *a* Savior and king,' and 'Christ is *my* Savior and *my* king.' But just how difficult this is, is indicated by the disciples, who scarcely believe that Christ is raised—not to mention that he is raised for them.

The godless people, who laugh at us when we preach the faith, do not know what faith is and does. They are blind fools and look at the resurrection like a cow staring at a new gate. But when you put your faith in his works, then he is such a champion, giant and hero, who had arrayed against him the gates of hell, all devils with their cunning, and death with all its powers. If they had considered this, they would not laugh so at us. Certainly we must learn it from our own experience that no one on earth, not even the emperor, can withstand death, and yet a Christian can do it. Therefore one must regard the resurrection with other than physical eyes; otherwise one has no comfort from it. Here one must open the eyes of the heart.

You have heard in the Passion how Christ let himself be crucified and buried and how sin and death trampled him underfoot. Satan and the sins of the world lie on him in the tomb. Sin, death and the devil are his lord. Therefore you must look into his tomb and realize that my sins and my death tear him apart and oppress him. There the devil regards himself as secure, and the chief priests boast and rejoice: He is gone and will not return. But in the instant when they believe him destroyed, the Lion tears himself away from sin, death, hell, and the jaws of the devil and rips them to shreds with his teeth. This is our comfort, that Christ comes forth: Death, sin, and the devil cannot hold him. The sin of the entire world is powerless. When he appears to Mary Magdalene, one sees in him neither death nor sin nor sadness but sheer life and joy. There I see that the Lord is mine and treads on the devil. Then I find my sins, torment, and devil where I ought to find them. There is the seed of the woman, who has struck the head of the serpent (Gen. 3:15), and says: Death, you shall die; Hell, you shall be defeated! Here is the victor.

It is a Christian art when a person can regard the Lord Jesus as the one whose business it is to deal with our sins. But if a sermon comes along that goes like this: You have sinned; you must do this and that and by your own works take action against those sins! Then they pit us against death and sin and call us to struggle against them with our works. Look how they teach us to regard sin and death: namely, that they are the strongest and rule in my conscience. There they lead me, a wretched person, so miserably alone against the devil.

Is this not a devil's sermon and a blasphemy against God and Christ? So if my works do it, I do not need Christ who died and is raised. When Satan and sin are there and you regard them as I have just described, then you are lost. Whenever you feel sin, death, plague, and attack of the devil, you can be given no assistance, save that you abandon what your conscience says and turn to Christ. You must say: Flesh and devil do not lay my sins in the right place; there they are too strong for me. But Christ is not raised for himself but for me, and the Scripture says that the sins of all people are laid on him, "Here is the Lamb of God who takes away the sin of the world" (John 1:29). There they lie! And let them lie there, where the Scripture puts them! If the devil wants to convince you otherwise, then just remember this sermon!

When the sins lie on Christ, then I see what the world, the devil, and sin do to him in the grave and in death: they hang on him and crush him; thus they are strong and devour him. But because today he now comes forth from the grave and remains in honor and glory, everything that the devil, sin, and death have done is destroyed. It is easy to say such words, but still no one believes it. It is truly a difficult article to believe, to stand with certainty on what I say, that all sins that I feel are not mine, that the fear of death is not mine. This is said contrary to all reason. But the Scripture certainly does not lie when it says that my sins lie on him. If this is true then they do not lie on me. Thus I must follow the logic of these utterances and say: I know nothing of sin, death, or the devil, for I look upon Christ. If they have not strangled him, then they must be dead. For when sin and death were capable of something, then I would expect to detect it in Christ. But they do nothing to him. He lives, I see no marks on him. For this reason they must be blown away like dust by the wind. Therefore a Christian ought to feel nothing of sin and death but look only upon Christ. Whoever can believe this article is a Christian.

But there Satan sees to it that such things do not come into our hearts; for he does not like it when anyone believes Satan's authority and power are nothing. And yet it is true: a believer has no sin and is lord over sin. Therefore when his authority and weapons have been scattered so that he has been reduced to nothing, do you think he feels good when he hears: You have tortured and killed Christ; now you get what you deserve? For this reason the devil resists when the resurrection is preached. The princes and kings with their swords and the wisest and most learned papists, heretics, and fanatics with their doctrine are obliged to assemble, for the devil knows that when Christians no longer look at sin and death on their own but only in Christ then he cannot keep Christ down. Then Christ is his Lord and the devil lies under his feet. When the devil sees those who believe, then he has much more work on his hands. Where the fire of faith threatens to break out, there he afflicts them in that moment, makes even good works to be sin, and always keeps the people in his sight.

Is it not a terrible thing that Satan can see to it that the Gospel is not preached? Then he rushes into the heart and rages so that one does not believe. For whoever believes knocks him flat with a snap of the fingers. It grieves him that a person, who is flesh and blood, should despise him and triumph over sin and death.

But our fanatics and papists do not know what faith is; they have no temptations, instead the devil lures them into regarding themselves as saints. But if they had the world with its wisdom and the devil dead set against them as we do, they would think differently. Indeed the more you look at the sin in you, the weaker Christ is in you. The less you look at the sin in you and see it only in Christ, the stronger Christ is in you. The apostles taught (2 Peter 3:18) it is an art you have to learn until the day you die, namely, that each day you trust in Christ. Wherever a Christian is there are always temptations, as Paul says, " I die daily" (1 Corinthians 15:31). In such a case I should say to the devil: I don't know of any sin, but there is Christ. On his neck hang the sins; you are wrong to place them on my heart, because God and the Scripture have bound them to Christ, to whom I look as the one who has no sin and yet has my sins.

This is our chief article which we must emphasize at all times and learn. And I have it not on my authority alone, but also have experienced it in others, that the devil works hard to tear this picture from our hearts. The Turks appear much holier than we do because they show love. The devil can tolerate this fine and even gives them considerable self-control, as he has also done with our priests and monks. This is all ours. When he maintains these things, then he has already won because the right picture is gone, namely, Christ who crawls through death to life.

For this reason he indeed lets righteous people alone, but Christians he cannot tolerate, namely, those who turn away from good and evil and depend on Christ. This is why the devil says: The Lord will reward you for good works and will condemn you for evil ones. When an evil conscience and fear plague Christians, then they say: This does not matter to me for I have no sins; Christ has them all. I see them there. He took them on himself on the cross and buried them. But now he lives and is risen. Indeed I have sins and good works, but I do not look at them; I look upon Christ alone. If they teach us that we become righteous through our works, they tear this picture from our hearts and slander Christ. And yet it is true: I am a sinner, and I am not a sinner. But they say: I only want to have good works. But if I didn't confess to being a sinner, I would not have Christ and would not be in need of him because I refused to be a sinner. For this reason, if I won't be a sinner, then I am one; and conversely, if I am in myself a condemned sinner but go outside myself and into Christ, then I am not one.

Christians from their own standpoint are a Judas, a Caiaphas, a Pilate and find themselves condemned. But there is another Person who took my sins on himself. On Good Friday they are all laid around his neck. But on Easter I also look at him, and then he has none. He has commanded that I look at my sins not on me, but on Christ. Whoever can do this has recovered from the snakes' bite [John 3:15] and looks at Christ rightly; for where there is no sin there is righteousness and life.

Thus sin is completely taken away in the resurrection. Everyone should learn this today, that all of us should abandon thoughts about ourselves and should not pass judgment on ourselves according to our feelings. For this is contrary to Christ and the Gospel, which says Christ has taken away the sin from our hearts and consciences and laid them on himself. For this reason the apostles praise the resurrection unceasingly. We should also do it because the flesh is too evil, Satan too powerful, and the conscience too slow for us to learn to look at Christ and not ourselves.

This is enough from the text for this morning. We must now call upon the Lord.

Endnotes

[1] In Luther's translation of this verse, the word "fear" (*erschrickt*) could also be translated "startled" which suggested to Luther a shaking of the earth itself.

[2] Contrary to the English translations, Luther's German version of this text has the disciples setting out on a second journey from Jerusalem, this time with the other women, but not with Mary Magdalene.

[3] Quoting from the hymn he had published in 1524, "Christ Is Arisen" (LBW 136; LuW 124). See also LW 53:255–57.

Easter Sunday Afternoon
March 28, 1529
The Resurrection of Christ as Proclamation

    This morning you heard the story of the Lord's resurrection from the dead that happened on this day, and how it is not enough just to hear and know it and regard it merely as a story. If it remains simply a work done for itself, then it does no one any good. Instead it has to be preached and acknowledged as a treasure and gift that each one receives just as if it happened to him or her, so that you, when you are asked, can tell what Christ has done today. Here your answer must be something more than: Christ is risen today. For the devil also knows as much, and even the godless papists preach it everywhere.

But a Christian must say more, namely, Christ did one other thing when he rose from the dead. What's that? With his resurrection Christ has brought about the following: He scattered and chased away the devil, he caused sin and all evil to disappear, and he made it so that the devil can dwell nowhere but remains all alone. I repeat such things again and again: This is our art; this is it. If I were Christ, I would command all apostles and preachers to preach this most diligently. For there are many who know the story well, and precisely for their sake I would like it to be preached. For they know it only according to the words.

Our sermon is: Christ's resurrection is not something that has to do with law or medicine; it is a treasure. Whoever does not look at Christ in this way does not know him. With his resurrection Christ brought about salvation and forgiveness of sins, as we sing, "Christ our comfort true will be."[1] But he cannot become this if you do not know what he has brought about with his resurrection. This is what the world does not know. But when I become so very glad about it, as it says in the same hymn, "Let our joy rise full and free," that is a completely different teaching from the world's preacher. When the preacher only says, "Christ is risen," this is of as much use to me as if I were to hear about a wealthy prince. Of what use is that to me? When you read: Christ is risen, then add: I with him and you with him. In this way we pull the resurrection into ourselves and ourselves into it. Whoever does not learn this, learns nothing at all. For this reason the teaching of the Gospel is different from that of Moses and all other teachers, who teach how one must live but say nothing about what is given to us.

That's why you hear about how the devil opposes this preaching: He can tolerate everything except this, that you receive this gift. But Christians know that they have everything Christ has. And Paul can speak about this best of all, as if Christ had not been raised but we had, except that he allows Christ the glory because he is the head who has done it for us (Ephesians 1:22; Colossians 2:10). This is what we should preach today.

But the Gospel shows in one text after another how difficult it is to believe these things. But all who do believe or could believe that it is true that they are raised from the dead and are lords over death and the devil, are called kings, indeed God himself. Those who believe it have already proved it; they have had their fight with the devil and with disease.[2]

But the work of the resurrection remains so secret that no one would have found out about, had the angels from heaven not come and proclaimed it. And it is made known to the very weakest people on earth—to women. We have often spoken of this part: that the Gospel is the vehicle or the means through which such knowledge comes. There sure would be a lot to say about the external Word over against the fanatics who despise it and only cry: Spirit! Spirit! The Spirit must be there![3] They are unable to recall that they learned that Christ suffered, died and rose through the Word. If they had not heard the external Word and read it in the Scripture, then they would have no knowledge of it. Having crossed this bridge themselves they now want to throw others into the gorge. Look here: Christ, after he was raised, could also have given the women the Holy Spirit without oral preaching. The work was there, and the women came to that place, went and found the tomb empty, and discovered that Christ is truly risen.

The work of Christ's resurrection is thus quite certainly true. But the disciples and the women explain it according to their reason: "They have carried him away." Do you see what reason does? Although the work is right in front of their eyes, if the Word is not added, then the tomb remains empty. But the Jews did not carry him away, and Christ is certainly risen and lives. There is nothing lacking in the work; only the Word still has to come to the rescue. As long as the Word is not spoken, they cannot understand the work. God has shown us his grace in that in the Word he has combined for us his works and the treasure, namely, that we are lords over the devil. Whoever wants to search without the Word will only find an empty tomb as the women and the disciples did. Then Christ would still be dead and carried away, and we would neither find him nor see him in all eternity.

For this reason honor the Holy Scripture! Christ did not want to appear to anyone at his resurrection: speaking the oral word had to be prior to everything else, and lest it happen without the Word, the angels came from heaven. No one should try to understand Christ except through the Word. The papists and the fanatics are opposed to it. Among them no one knows anything of Christ's resurrection. The angel is the first one who says it, so the oral Word must come first. The fanatics err in that they don't consider where they have learned about the resurrection. Instead they follow only their own thoughts that the Holy Spirit speaks apart from the Word. To be sure, the insufferable Satan does! In conclusion: We will never experience who Christ is and the treasure he brings with him if it is not proclaimed in the Sunday sermon or in encouragement given in the home!

For this reason the words of the angel read: "Why do you look for the living among the dead?" [Luke 24:5]. This is evangelical preaching, which the angels begin so wonderfully. Do not seek Christ among the dead! "He is not here, but has risen." He is over the dead; he has risen much higher. The dead are those who are under the law and their works. There you dare not seek Christ. But our reason loves to seek Christ with its own works, as St. Gregory observed: "The women sought Christ with fine ointments, therefore we must seek him with good works."[4] But the angel says: You will not find him in this way! And he rebukes their search. All who come with their own works have Christ as a dead corpse. For them he is not risen, but is dead. They think they themselves should do something good and do not want to have him as a helper.

For this reason the angel rebukes the women. How? He says: I proclaim to you that he is risen! The word indicates to them that he is not among the dead but that he is risen. This is the preaching of the Gospel, that Christ is found not with works but through the hearing of the Word, not with meditation but through the sermon. The works of the women are indeed good, but the Word is lost with them. If one wants to make a Christian righteous through his or her works, then things will be only all the more wicked.

This article of faith is not for the masses, but is a sermon for Christians. The highly learned teachers in the schools and the kings do not understand it. But Christians understand it since it applies to them. These are the people to whom I want to preach.

The women are just the same. Look, it had to happen that the resurrection of Christ was preached by the angel and to the women, that the men indeed would not be the first. The preacher is wonderful; there is no imperfection. It is not an apostle but an angel from heaven instead. He and his sermon lack nothing. Therefore our office of teaching is also not weak. The angel has power and wisdom enough. This had to be in order for them to be certain of his words. But the students—the poor, simple, frightened women, on whom the news broke—are silly fools. They all forgot the stone! They go to buy ointment as if they were going into a house where all the doors stand open. Then Mary says: What shall we do? We won't get anywhere with the guards there!

The Scripture says the man is stronger in courage and body than the woman.[5] The most glorious sermon of the angel is made known to the weakest vessel. It is the holy Gospel even if it is not preached to the men! Those who should hear it are such foolish people. It is a wonderfully strong, certain sermon that never fails. That is, there is nothing lacking in Christianity's teacher or its teaching, but the students are poor, wretched people. It is an amazing thing that a person be led away from her or his life, even from the very best, in order to hold only to the one who is risen from the dead. The Word is powerful, certain, and sure because the angel has spoken it. But Magdalena remains Magdalena, the same with Johanna and Salome. Indeed, we are children, poor and weak students, who do not think that teaching is worth much, although it is worthy to have nothing but angels in the audience. But we behave toward it as weak, crazy, and foolish people. It is a great comfort that the womenfolk are the model of those who hear the Gospel and of those to whom it is preached. Even though they are so weak, it is nevertheless preached to them.

After the sermon the Lord appears to them. Then you see in these same women a marvelous, invincible strength that they have from the Word, which stands firm against all the attacks of the devil. But the women are crazy and foolish in and of themselves. Therefore weakness and power, riches and poverty meet and get baked together. For those who receive the Gospel are Magdalenas, that is, they are weak, and yet the Word that they hear tears through death and sin.

Thereby the Evangelist wanted to indicate that the Gospel brings us such a great treasure, though we are also weak, as long as one does not struggle against it. Mary means a "drop in the sea"; Magdalene means "a good, solid, strong tower."[6] That's why John names Mary Magdalene, for the sake of her name alone. She is a Mary, that is, she is not a bucket full of water, but only a little drop; that is, she is nothing at all, and yet she is a Magdalene, that is, she has a tower from which she can be so strong. As Solomon says, "The name of the Lord is a strong tower; the righteous run into it and are safe" (Proverbs 18:10). She carries the name Magdalene: a tower does such solid things that no one can conquer it. Yet she is also Mary: a "drop in the sea," a droplet.

For ourselves we are only a poor little drop of water. Satan has a heap of tongues and would guzzle down half the Elbe. And yet he is so weak that he cannot do it, for he will find a tower there. The Word, which the angel carries, is the power. For this reason let us take care that we stick with the Word. The other Mary is the mother of James (meaning: one who takes shelter), and Salome (meaning: a source of peace). All names are connected to their disposition. So the women are not led in vain by the Holy Spirit, so that although they are the weakest students, nevertheless they are by far the strongest.

Therefore a Christian should know what this resurrection effects in the weak. For this reason the Gospel first had to become clear to the women and then come to the apostles. It caused them trouble because it is so high and glorious that reason cannot grasp it. If this had been said, "Fast to St. Barbara!" everyone would easily understand it. But instead this is said, "All that you do is nothing but foolishness and women's work." The women wanted to anoint the Lord and didn't find him! The world cannot tolerate that the ointments we prepare with such great works should be nothing. For this reason the angel says, "Why do you look for the living among the dead?" But the situation is this: He is risen. Then hold on to this! I have proclaimed it to you.

Even our enemies preach Christ is risen from the dead and also carry Paul's word in their mouths: "who was handed over for our trespasses and raised for our justification" (Rom. 4:25). I hope they will do this. But the conclusions overthrow them: If this is true that Christ with his resurrection has set us free from sin, death, and devil, then I cannot do it. Therefore it is not necessary that the priest reads masses for the dead and that I atone for myself with innumerable works. But this they do not tolerate but want to maintain both things at the same time by saying, "You must also do your part." But Paul teaches the conclusion that is called Christian freedom. If I believe that Christ has taken my sins upon himself, then I cannot take them on myself. But if I take them on myself, then Christ does not have them. If Christ has taken them on himself then he is not the kind of savior who requires my help. Indeed if he needs my help, then he is a poor fellow and we would need a different Christ.

But now they do not tolerate this conclusion that Paul indicates. It must follow: If Christ takes away my sins why do I run to the monastery and become a Carthusian? But you say: I have bought a mass; I have done this and that work; are these all for nothing? That's a mess we can't get out of and so must remain in.

This is the sign that they only talk about Christ and his resurrection and only sing about them. But you must keep it. Now they say: If you do not keep the command of the church about fasting, festivals, receiving one kind in the Lord's Supper, remaining in the monastery, then you are condemned. Yet they preach the resurrection of Christ at the same time! How does this fit together? I respond that even when what God has commanded ("You shall not kill" and the like) is required and I fulfill them, I nevertheless do not become saved. Why do you teach me that I am saved when I receive the Lord's Supper in one kind and the like? Only Christ can help us. If I can be saved through obedience to the church and human ordinances, then I want to give Christ a vacation.

People do not want to tolerate or hear this at all. We also teach that a person's outward life should be honorable but not that we thereby become righteous. If you want to be a monk, no one is going to stop you. But that you want to atone for your sins with the cowl, then what has that One done about whom you sing and preach: "who was handed over for our trespasses and raised for our justification" (Romans 4:25)? They cannot tolerate the conclusion. For this reason Paul says "If Christ has not been raised, . . . you are still in your sins" (1 Corinthians 15:17). For this reason as much as you might like to try and get out from under your sins, you can't do it; only the resurrection of Christ can do it. When you say: That person lived as a upstanding citizen and will go to heaven—sure, to a make-believe heaven!

This article destroys everything that people preach about spiritual, holy estates, brotherhoods, pilgrimages, and all the other works a person does. All these works have no more worth than good, old foolish Mary Magdalene who comes trotting along, her pots full of ointment, and yet hears from the angel: You are a fool to seek the Lord among the dead since you should seek him out there among the living. You do not know where you are going! Therefore one should praise the works of the dear holy women in this way. Before God and the world and themselves and even the angels they act foolishly. Here's how these women are pictured: Their intention and their work is good and yet it does them no good until they come to the hearing of the Gospel. In addition they fret over these things until they received the Gospel. Then they forget the jars and the ointments, get out of themselves and become strong.

I want all preachers to deal properly with this article. Most of them stand there and do not know what to say. I, too, am still a weak student of this teaching. I, too, cling to the jars and the godless ointment and the tomb and cannot get out from under them. But that's the way God wants it. The sermon is certain; only the disciples are weak. This really is a comfort to us so that we do not despair even when we do not understand it. Certainly the women should have said, "O God be praised!" But instead of this they hang their heads and think, "Is it true or not?"

Endnotes

[1] A reference to the Easter sequence, much loved by Luther, "Christ Is Arisen" (LBW 136; LuW 124): "Christ is arisen from the grave's dark prison. So let our joy rise full and free; Christ our comfort true will be. Alleluia!"

[2] Cf. Mark 16:17f.

[3] Here Luther is reacting against certain spiritualists, like Hans Denck, or his former colleague, Andreas Bodenstein von Karlstadt, who attacked Luther for sticking too closely to the external word and ignoring the Spirit.

[4] Gregory the Great, *Homiliae in Evangelia,* 21 (PL 76:1170).

[5] Cf. 1 Peter 3:7 and Luther's comments on this text from 1523 (LW 30:91–93).

[6] Luther derives these etymologies from Jerome, *De nominibus Hebraicis* (PL 23:789). The words Luther uses (*Schloß* and *Turm*) are reminiscent of "Ein' feste Burg" ("A Mighty Fortress" LBW 229; LuW 297).

Easter Monday Morning
March 29, 1529
The Resurrection of Christ and Dying to the Law

Yesterday you first heard the story, to which this text (Luke 24:13ff.) also belongs because it also occurred on Easter. Then you heard what one should learn and believe regarding the resurrection of the Lord and what is the blessing and treasure that benefit us. Further, you heard how difficult it is to believe not because of the work in itself—for this is certain and is proclaimed—but because no one has seen it and before it is seen it is accomplished only through the Word. This is difficult to believe because the persons are so weak.

"The sun had not yet risen," that is: It was still a dark understanding or an idle tale.[1] Most people still regard it as a idle tale, although they also sing and confess with the rest. Nevertheless, it most likely remains a idle tale to them. Satan and the opposition of the world help with the result that Satan and the world and the chief priests are opposed to it, resist with all their might, and give the soldiers money so that this work of the resurrection might not be true.

Concerning the stone, Mark says that "It was very large" (Mark 16:4). This also opposes the resurrection. The stone signifies the unbelief in our hearts, that we cannot believe Christ is risen, as one says in German, "It weighs on my heart as if a stone lay on it," that is, if I did not have this burden, I could believe. Further the guards and the seal are there so that no one may touch the stone. To the poor women Christ is by no means dead, although they do not know it, but to the Jews he is quite dead. The guards are Levites, that is, the priests who have preached the Law and therefore killed Christ. For it is the belief of the Jews and the Turks that they do not need Christ's labors. As they also say, the Lord never was raised, but the disciples came and stole his body.

Thus they have the empty tomb, that is, an empty Scripture, always staring and yet not wanting to confess him who lay in there, whom they killed. Therefore the large stone remains on their hearts. But for Christians it is opened and the seal is broken. The large stone is rolled away and now the Scripture concerning Christ is attested to us. All the dungeons, in which they imprisoned the conscience and bound Christ, are broken open. The law cannot imprison Christians. A Christian is over the Law and works, has the gift of Christ's resurrection which is not under the Law but is well over the Law. Christ is not indebted to the Law but is Lord over it. If we are Christians, Paul says (Colossians 3:1), then we are raised with Christ. Why should we then let ourselves be imprisoned with laws?

Even today we struggle against the pope because we allow no law to be laid on our conscience. The pope and his followers are like the Jews: for them Christ lies dead on account of the works that burden the people. Even if Christ's resurrection is still preached, he nevertheless remains dead to them. But no law ought to be laid on a Christian's conscience. I'm not talking about flesh and blood,[2] for the godless understand from this sermon that they need to do nothing. But in the flesh I should be subject to all laws, parents, a Christian government, and yet in my conscience I am subject to no law. Instead, I am to soar high above all commands. Otherwise a person does not understand the resurrection of Christ, that the stone is rolled away, the tomb open and the seals broken. Christ was not imprisoned under the "stone,"[3] and neither are Christians. Christians should never allow this stone to lie over their hearts. One must not make Christ a law professor, as the pope has done.

This sounds like complete make-believe in the ears of those who do not understand the faith. For a Christian is supposed to believe that sin is drowned in Christ, that Christ has come forth and destroyed sins. But if Christians remain under the Law, then they also remain under sin and death. Therefore everything must be put aside together. Paul is very capable of explaining this matter for Christians, and I desire that all preachers would emphasize this article with great diligence like Paul, so that the conscience could be free of death, sin, and Satan in the kingdom of Heaven, as Christ says to the thief, "Today you will be with me in paradise" (Luke 23:43). If sin is not abolished then neither is death. But in fact sin is abolished by Christ. And if sin is abolished, then so is the Law, for the Law causes sin.

As long as the feeling of sin remains in a person, just as long will the Law rule in the human heart if the "stone" is not taken away from the tomb. The Law must be taken away from Christians, that is, their conscience must not be afflicted by the Law which makes them feel ashamed. But the Law belongs at the place where it says: You jackass! Thou shalt not! But in the conscience Christ is risen from sin, death, Law and from the "stone," since he is over all things that can burden the human conscience. In so far as a conscience feels thorns and burdens, it is lacking in faith.

When Christ rises, the stone of the Law still remains until the angel comes and indicates through preaching that it is taken away and he sits on top of it. According to the flesh you are a servant of all laws, even the bad ones as Christ says, "And if anyone wants to sue you and take your coat, give your cloak as well" (Matthew 5:40). This sermon is not for the old nature. The fanatics assume that it applies to the freedom of the flesh. But Christians endure all external things; only in the conscience are they free and acknowledge the resurrection of Christ, that Christ is over all. They learn through the resurrection that they no longer have a burdened conscience, for the conscience feels and knows what is not true and is against Christ. But the stone is gone. You think perhaps you believe Christ. But the stone and the voice of the angel say otherwise: "Why do you look for the living among the dead?" Still you feel as if he were dead, that is, why do you believe you are a sinner and under the Law? You still act as if Christ were still in the tomb. But now "you were also raised with him" as Colossians 2:12 says, in order that no one may be over your conscience.

If the pope says: In Lent eat fish but no meat by obedience and the ban! then answer: Sure, I can do this so that I impose it on my old Adam, but I refuse to impose it on my conscience. There my conscience should remain free; there is another Man who helps me. If I keep your commands, I will not be better for it and if I break them, none the worse. But I will do it for your sake, just as when Moses says, Obey your parents! Sure, I will do it, I will gladly impose it on my old Adam. But if you want me to impose it on my conscience, there I will not let you enter! I will not allow the "stone" to lie on my heart. If I am obedient to my parents, then I am not better for it.

In the same way, if I am no longer under their authority, then I am not worse off for it. "One thing is necessary" (Luke 10:42). There is One who has set the conscience free from all other laws. If it is necessary, then I will do it to the extent that my conscience not be forced. Otherwise I will tear the seal in pieces and cast away the stone, with which they want to burden my conscience. I will not tolerate the stone, which has been rolled away, to be laid again before the tomb. For by saying, If you do this you will be saved, they want to turn me away from Christ, so that I deny him. But I would rather deny the pope. If my parents laid on me the obedience for the sake of conscience, I would say, For this reason I will not be obedient, because you draw obedience into the conscience of a Christian.

In conclusion: There should be no other comfort or certainty than, as you sing, "Christ our comfort true will be."[4] For this reason I cannot tolerate that something else is put next to Christ in my conscience. With many words I impress it on you: The Christians' teaching is to learn to distinguish between hand and heart. We do not make the hand free but lay many laws on it. But the heart knows of no command because it has died to all of these. Because Christ, who committed no sin and has cast down all things, is risen, so we also are free: If the devil can accuse Christ of no sin, then he also cannot accuse me. If Christ is not subject to anything, then neither are we, for his resurrection is ours. Everything depends on our learning that Christ's resurrection is mine. Then it can be concluded that if it can't happen to Christ, it can't happen to me.

But what is lacking is faith. The women and the apostles are weak, and the sun is not yet risen for them. In conclusion: a Christian is to be happy constantly, as Paul says, "Rejoice in the Lord always" (Philippians 4:4). To the other people Christ is dead although he is risen. Because they do not see how Christ's resurrection is ours, they cannot understand it and do not trouble themselves about it. For this reason they remain hypocrites filled with works righteousness. Thus even the Turk leads a beautiful life, except for whoredom.[5]

But away with your holiness, like the thief on the cross! Indeed the thief belongs in the kingdom of heaven through the Word: "Today you will be with me in paradise!" Thereby he enters into paradise. He lets his body and his righteousness hang on the cross. Therefore he is in paradise with Christ through his resurrection. That thief goes beyond the righteousness that is on earth—otherwise the other thief would also have been saved—and clings to the one who is under no law. The earthly righteousness ceases and does not stand the test. But there must be One who is eternally over death and devil. For this reason Paul will not tolerate that Christians be perplexed in the conscience. It is the greatest skill: a Christian must be protected so that no one nails a law to her or his conscience and heart. You must have this skill if you want to believe in Christ. This is over all laws. If a hundred thousand sins fell on you today, you would still have to say, I know of none because Christ, who is subject to neither sin nor death, is risen from the dead.

If reason could only regard this as true, it would have to reflect on Christ, not on itself, and say: If my Christ has neither sin nor punishment nor death, then I do not have it either. In the body is punishment, but reason wishes immediately to escape. If someone could create "a firmament between the upper and lower water" (Genesis 1:6) then the conscience may say, I cannot commit sin, as John says, "Whoever is born of God does not sin" (1 John 3:9). Being a Christian and committing sin is impossible! Why? Christ cannot sin and his resurrection is mine. But if Christians feel that they sin, then Christ is dead to them.

This is said of the "stone," that is, of our conscience which deceives us and aids the world and the pope. And the pope also leaves his mark on it, as is written in Revelation 13:16, and regards Christ as dead. And just as the guards accuse the disciples of having stolen Christ's body, so the papists revile us so that to them we must be the thieves who steal Christ and veil the Scripture. And as they gave the soldiers ample money, so the pope gives ample money and cardinal hats. To become rich immediately, they want to write against us that we interpret the Scripture falsely. Thus it continues up to this day that he is taken away. So the papists see that he is taken away, but say that we put on a pretense. We get no money, but the "Carrotspoons"[6] take it and write what people like to hear, that we must be the falsifiers of Scripture.

As Paul says, "Through the law I have died to the law so that I might live to God" (Gal. 2:19), that is, I know neither sin nor law. Just as Christ is not troubled by pope or emperor but is a lord over all, so am I, too, according to the conscience and heart, but not according to the body. It is a sermon of comfort for the conscience that one not let Christ remain in the tomb under the stone.

Endnotes

[1] In this sermon Luther employs allegory to apply the meaning of the resurrection for his hearers. Luther employed allegory throughout his life as an aid to preaching and biblical interpretation. He rejected wild allegory not based in faith and God's Word, and he avoided using allegory in theological debate.

[2] Here and in the next sermon Luther touches upon the substance of a dispute between two teachers within the evangelical camp who had been his students: John Agricola, teacher at the Latin school in Eisleben, and Philip Melanchthon. In 1527 Agricola had attacked the Saxon Visitation Articles (instructions for the official visitors of the churches in Saxony written by Melanchthon and revised by Luther) on grounds that they reintroduced the medieval understanding of penitence and taught that sorrow for sin arose out of the preaching of the Law, not the Gospel. Luther sided with Melanchthon but managed to reconcile the two men. Only ten years later did Agricola's full-fledged antinomianism lead to a final break with Luther.

[3] Literally: "was not imprisoned under the *quippe*." Luther is referring to the Latin translation of Mark 16:4, "Erat quippe magnus valde" ("it was *indeed* very large"). We have followed the suggestion of Mülhaupt, p. 364 note 154, and translated it as "stone."

[4] A reference to the Easter sequence, "Christ is Arisen" (LBW 136; LuW 124).

[5] Luther is thinking of the practice of polygamy.

[6] Luther's nickname for John Cochlaeus, the court theologian for Duke George of Saxony, who paid him to write against Luther. See above, p. 60 note 7.

Easter Monday Afternoon
March 29, 1529
The Resurrected Christ Appears to Mary Magdalene (John 20:11–18)

This morning we heard the Gospel that is supposed to be dealt with now (Luke 24:13ff.). But first we want to speak further of the preceding stories. John writes how Mary Magdalene remained at the tomb, saw the Lord, but thought he was the gardener until the Lord let his voice be heard and called Mary by name. Then she recognized him, fell down before him, and wanted to touch his feet as was her custom. But the Lord says, "Do not hold on to me because I have not yet ascended to the Father" (John 20:17). Now we have to preach about that.

You heard yesterday and today that the story of Christ's resurrection is made known through the Word alone. The angels proclaimed it to the women, who in turn proclaimed it to the apostles. And yet, without faith this Word is preached in vain. Even had the women believed, the disciples would still have called it an idle tale. Thus even today it remains an idle tale when this does not follow: that Christ himself appears and lets himself be heard. However it only helps so much. He appears to Mary Magdalene, to the women, to Peter—and still it remains an idle tale, as Thomas says, "Unless I see the mark of the nails in his hands, and put my finger in the mark of the nails and my hand in his side, I will not believe" (John 20:25).

Even if we admit to all other doctrines, when this article about Christ's resurrection does not entirely penetrate our hearts, the Gospel will not stick. This teaching is not only talked about, but the Lord also appears, and yet it does not help at all except among his Christians. That is: the Gospel is preached, the Lord appears in addition and lets himself be seen by the apostles and still something is lacking. That is, the Gospel proceeds with difficulty and is opposed by the devil. But nevertheless comfort is present as here in this text. When it is preached by the angel and the women, it does not remain external. The Lord follows and appears, that is, the Spirit himself follows hard on his heels.

And this is our boast against the enthusiasts who say the Gospel is only a letter and oral word.[1] It is indeed true: the word which the angel and the women speak is an oral word. But from this Word it follows that the Lord himself appears to Mary Magdalene, to the disciples, to Peter, and to the women. Certainly he does not remain external where the Word is preached. So also in today's Gospel: When the disciples begin to speak, he is not far off. That is, the Word does not leave without bearing fruit—no matter who would prevent and inhibit it.

For this reason each one should gladly hear the Gospel, for the fruit will not fail to appear. Mary Magdalene has the Word, and the women and the disciples have the Word and, although they also doubt, the Lord nevertheless comes to them. Only let us not listen to the guards and fanatics who take away the Word from us! If you only cling to the "idle tale"—no matter what you are like—then it will not leave without bearing fruit, and Christ will come to you as he appeared to Mary Magdalene. But if we have lost the Word, we imagine that we are no longer weak, but altogether strong. The story wants to say this: that Mary Magdalene indeed heard the sermon and yet remained weak. But since it was nevertheless the Word, the Lord appeared to her.

Let us listen only to the true preacher who says, "Do not hold on to me!" Whoever wants to hear a sermon, listen to this! But that the text reads, "because I have not yet ascended to the Father," I am not able to interpret as thoroughly as is necessary. Some[2] interpret the words in this way: Christ did not want to be touched because Mary Magdalene did not yet believe. She thought he was coming back to the life in which he was previously and was therefore supposed to stay with them. Christ wants to say: No longer am I to be touched as friends tend to do it. I do not need your ointment.³ Thus with these words he says farewell to all things on earth. The point is that Christ is gone, as Isaiah 53:8 says: "He is cut off from the land of the living." A distinction is made between Christ and this world. They are separate.

This text necessarily goes along with what I have said earlier today—only without confusion!⁴ "Do not hold on to me!" For you are still under law and sin; I do not like you; I cannot abide you. This is a deep sermon. There is a great distinction between Christ and a worldly person: there is no contact between them, no reconciling them, they do not belong together. But afterwards when the other women came, he allowed himself to be touched (Matthew 28:9). The Christian life does not consist in how one obeys one's parents: that belongs on the earth and does not reach up to heaven. To be sure, one should do it and Christ even commands it! However, he says: This has nothing to do with me. I have greater things to do. Why? Answer: " I have not yet ascended to my Father."

John has added this so that one may not search for a host of explanations for why he does not allow himself to be touched. As far as his person was concerned, he was already gone to the Father, but for the sake of your person he had not yet ascended. I cannot preach as I really would like to. I cannot sufficiently develop the work of the resurrection of Christ in us, and yet Christ speaks all these words for our benefit. In other words, he could also have said: "Do not hold on to me because I have not yet ascended for you." For Mary Magdalene had not yet renounced earthly things completely and thrown herself entirely on Christ. Christ will distribute his resurrection to us. He uses "I" with Mary Magdalene so that a Christian may always allow the third and first person singular to be a unity and combine them so that Christ will not be regarded simply for his person, but as the Lamb of God who takes away our sins. For this reason when Christ says "I," we should always consider that it concerns us.

Therefore in this text Mary Magdalene and all who are in the flesh are sent away—and yet she is not yet rejected. She should still be obedient because she still walks on earth and has to work. But he is higher as the following text indicates:

"But go to my brothers" [John 20:17]. To that one it was farewell. There he had bluntly refused to have anything to do with us. But now he says "Go to my brothers." The two are completely contradictory. First he will not let himself be touched and now he wants to be a brother. So if we are his brothers and sisters, we must not only touch him but embrace him. It is an amazing sermon! First he says, "Mary Magdalene, rise, I do not like you," and then he calls her his dear sister. This was nicely said. For this reason set the text in golden letters, because in it is the Gospel. I cannot preach it as it deserves. "Say to them, 'I ascend to my Father and your Father, to my God and to your God'" [John 20:17]. Pay heed to what is said here: Christ who died and was buried is now risen from the dead, has departed from this life, and has no brothers or sisters, indeed will recognize no one. There is obviously a clear distinction here: "I have no one on earth" and yet now he says: "my brothers." Thus a worldly and a heavenly nature must be joined together. Whoever wants to be a Christian, learn these words: they are "my brothers." Write this with the largest letters so that you know it.

What does a "brother" or "sister" mean? In the world it happens like this: If there are many brothers and sisters in a household, they are not very upset when one of them dies [because one then receives a greater inheritance]. But here Christ seeks his brothers and sisters. The disciples all fled from him and scarcely thought they were worthy to be his house servants (cf. Luke 15:19) because of their denial. O how happy they are now! They did not dare to expect so much from him. And he raises up Mary and says, "Go to my brothers and say to them," etc.

This Word should indeed raise 300,000 dead from under the earth. If only they could believe it! The words are there, one has only to believe. But how? Peter, who denied him, and the others fell away. By what means did they deserve it? With denials and apostasy! Compare the word "brother" with servant or gate keeper. If they are his brothers and sisters, then they sit on the same chair with like power and right, only that he is "the first born within a large family" (Romans 8:29), through whom all others will become such. They have equal right to the inheritance, that is: to the property. The "brother" brings that with him. If he is a "brother," then he is no lord, servant, or enemy.

Where in the Scripture can a more powerful statement than this be found? If the King of France or England were to say to me: "Come, you shall be my brother!" and said it earnestly, then I would think: "Whatever is done to the brothers of the king, must be done to me! Where the king sits, eats and sleeps, there can I do it, too." But what is lacking here is that no one considers who it is who is speaking this word in the Gospel. From this "brother" comes such a Lord that no one can comprehend it.

Then what is Christ? It is found here: The greatest glory lies in the word "my brothers" as Hebrews 2:11 says: "For this reason he is not ashamed to call them brothers and sisters." But if we are Christ's brothers and sisters, then we possess the same inheritance, property, and rights that he has—only with this exception, that we are not his person and nature. We are not Christ and yet sit in the midst of the same possessions and rights as he himself.[5] For this reason he is called "the firstborn within a large family" (Romans 8:29). Subsequently the others come after him, and yet they receive the same possessions although they do not have the same nature, for we are not by nature a Son of God but are set free from sins. But everything apart from his nature is ours, or else this text is lying.[6]

In worldly matters a person says: "Oh, I wish he were not my brother!" There no one is glad to have a lot of siblings, because each would like to have the inheritance for himself or herself. So it would have to come from the heart—from a free, upright heart—that someone would allow not only a brother or sister but even an enemy to partake in the inheritance. Indeed the world desires just the opposite, namely, that the brothers and sisters die. It is already considered as an extraordinarily great righteousness before God that one wishes they have life. But if one has the inheritance in hand and then says, "I want to regard you as brother, as sister, be like I am!" See, this is what Christ does: "Go and say to my brothers!" I am separated from you on earth; I am different, not mortal, but a Lord over death. In the words "my brothers" lies this: All that I have, all to which I have a right, that too you possess—except for Christ's person and nature.

Whoever could believe this would believe that they are a lord over all sin, death, and devil. If Christ received as brothers those who received the Word delivered to them by Mary Magdalene and believed that Christ has as a right over law and death, then a Christian is a defiant emperor over sin. This is what the word "my brothers" bestows: The Epistle to the Hebrews (2:11) praises this most highly: "For this reason Jesus is not ashamed to call them brothers and sisters." The author of Hebrews considered it carefully so that he based it all on the Word.[7]

So consider diligently that Christ says: "Do not hold on to me, I have not yet ascended." In sum he wants to say: Mary Magdalene, I am not yet regarded by you as I should be. You regard me as a lawgiver. You want to touch me with your works. But I am ascending so that you may learn to distinguish the physical nature on earth with all its righteousness from my nature. I am taking on a different nature and "I am ascending to my Father and your Father."

There he describes what kind of possessions, inheritance, and right he has, namely, "I am ascending," that is, I am Lord over all. No one will put the Father nor me under the law, sin, death, or devil, for I go to the Father. Whoever can overpower the Father, overpowers Christ and his brothers and sisters, too. Let the devil try! If Christ ascends to the Father, then the Father, Christ, and his brothers and sisters are baked in one cake. An excellent statement so that we know there must be something higher surrounding a Christian than that he or she knows only earthly things. When he says that he goes to his Father and to the Father of his brothers and sisters, then they must all be together in the heavenly kingdom, for they are siblings. Whoever can believe this is a Christian. If only we could believe that it is true, that we are Christ's brothers and sisters! Only that we do not hold on to him—for he says: "I do not want your things, but you, take my thing! You do not make me your brother, but I make you my brothers and sisters. You will not give me something, but the other way around."

Therefore Christians must in their hearts be over world, law, devil, and death, which must not touch them. If these things touch us, then we are no Christians. It reads "to the Father": He is a Lord over all so that nothing overpowers him and subsequently he is our brother. So consider who this is, who speaks this way and, then consider what he has for possessions. Therefore everything on earth having to do with good works and merits must not get tangled up with Christ, or you lose Christ as a brother. Therefore it is necessary that you seize this message and embrace his possessions and rights. There Paul is a master at interpreting these words, as in Colossians 2 (vs. 12ff.), and yet words fail even him. Think what the word "brother" or "sister" implies, and yet this is offered to people who are not family. A Christian who believes this must, on the basis of this text, be sure and happy. There is nothing lacking in these words that the Lord himself speaks and commands. What is lacking is our faith.

Endnotes

[1] Spiritualists like Hans Denck, who thought the Holy Spirit overcame the external Word, or Andreas Bodenstein von Karlstadt, who minimized the letter of Scripture in favor of the unmediated authority of the Spirit.

[2] This was especially the opinion of John Chrysostom in his *Homilies on the gospel of John* (NPNF, ser. 1, 14:324). At the same place in his *Tractates on John* Augustine emphasizes, as Luther does, the importance of faith (NPNF, ser. 1, 7:437–38).

[3] Cf. Luke 7:36–50 and 8:2. Luther, like most of his contemporaries, linked all these stories together as part of Mary Magdalene's life.

[4] See the previous sermon, where Luther allegorizes the text.

[5] Here Luther uses one of his favorite approaches to the atonement, the "joyous exchange," in which Christ exchanges his righteousness for the believer's sin. For example, see his tract, *The Freedom of a Christian* (LW 31:351–52).

[6] In a sermon from Easter Sunday, 5 April 1523, Luther expanded upon the idea of Christ as our brother and the inheritance which he provides. See Lenker 2:217ff.

[7] Cf. Hebrews 2:12–13, where the author quotes Psalm 22:22 and Isaiah 8:17–18.

Easter Tuesday Morning
March 30, 1529
The Resurrected Christ Commissions the Disciples (John 20:19–20)

You heard on these two days how the story and the work of the resurrection should be applied to us so that we receive it. This Gospel (John 20:21–29) does that, too. Here Christ commands his disciples to be confident because he is sent by the Father, and after that he gives them the Holy Spirit.

"If you forgive the sins of any, they are forgiven them; if you retain the sins of any, they are retained" [John 20:23]. We want to talk a little about this text. He says, "I send you" (v. 21), and gives them the Holy Spirit. Under the pope people dared to seize hold of the authority to forgive or retain sins without having preached the Gospel. The question arises whether people who do not have the Holy Spirit have the power to forgive sins. For here it is written: "Receive the Holy Spirit!" (v. 22). Christ did not want to establish such work without the Holy Spirit. However, what are we to make of those who do not have the Holy Spirit? That is also a great question today. Many take offense at it and say, "Rogues cannot preach the Gospel." The Donatists formerly came with this opinion and today the Anabaptists.[1] They are under the delusion that if the priest is ungodly, then he cannot preach the Gospel or administer the sacraments. Whoever is impure, so they say, cannot make others pure; whoever has unclean hands cannot wash the world clean.

Respond this way: It is most certainly true that the Holy Spirit's office belongs only to the Holy Spirit, and to the extent that the Holy Spirit is present, to that extent there is blood and sacrament. But the Gospel has always continued even among its opponents. The papists also preach the text, even if they fight against it and interpret it according to their own understanding as well. Nevertheless the text of Baptism and of the Sacrament of the Altar, the preaching office and the ordinance of the Holy Spirit have remained among them. To the extent these things are present, forgiveness of sins and Christ's gifts will also follow. For that reason, note to what extent the Holy Spirit is present or not. If the Gospel is preached, then the Spirit is present, even if a donkey preaches—as you have heard about Balaam who preached the Gospel and Word of God stiffly, though he was a godless person (Numbers 23 & 24). In the same way John speaks of Caiaphas (John 11:49–52), and even Saul was a prophet (1 Sam. 10:10ff.). One should not pay so much attention to the person as to the office. For the office remains, even though ungodly people abuse it. Therefore as far as you are concerned, to the extent a person deals with the Word in accord with proper order, to that extent the Holy Spirit and the forgiveness of sins are present. If it were based on our righteousness, then we would never become aware of God's gifts.

One can have the Holy Spirit in two different ways: first, for the individual so that he or she is justified, even if this person has no office to exercise as, for example, a daughter.[2] This is indeed the best way to have the Holy Spirit. And second, when someone does not have the Holy Spirit for himself, but for his office. Thus evil pastors, fanatics, and heretics do not have the Holy Spirit for themselves, but for their office. For the office does not belong to the ungodly, but to Christ, who has laid it on them: "If you forgive the sins of any they are forgiven; if you retain the sins of any, they are retained" (John 20:23).

So I owe also my parents obedience, if they deal with me according to their office. However, if they deal with me according to their person and their counsel forces me to godlessness, then they abuse their office according to their wantonness. So also I should obey the pastor to the extent he acts as the ordinance of Christ commands him. However, if he acts contrary to it, then I say: I allow you to issue the ban, but I do not worry much about it, for you thereby follow your wantonness and abuse it for personal gain. But if you do it in so far as the office commands you, so that you forgive the sins of this person or that one and absolve them, then I obey. So let each and everyone watch, whether their pastors govern them according to their wantonness or according to their office.

Here you must make a distinction between the fanatics and the true preachers. The judgment must stand with you. You must be certain about it when the preacher remains in his office and when he oversteps it. You have the Gospel. If he preaches according to the same, well and good! To preach the Gospel is his office. If he makes up his own creed, teaching, or article, then I say: that is not your office, but your wantonness and your own person. So you can tolerate this to some extent. It is true that no one who does not have the Holy Spirit in their office can forgive sins—but they do not do this on their own. For the office is not ours, does not belong to the person, but to the Holy Spirit and to Christ. And to the extent this is the case, to that extent the Holy Spirit is with the person concerned. It can indeed be that he does not have the Holy Spirit, in so far as the Spirit touches him personally, but only because of the office.

Thus Christ has given the Holy Spirit to Christianity and to every preacher and pastor so that they should teach, comfort, and admonish. If this were not so, then everything would be completely uncertain. I would have to be baptized anew again tomorrow, because I would not know whether the baptizer is faithful. For that reason people should close their eyes and commend each officeholder to his own conscience, whether he is righteous or not, whether he has the Holy Spirit or not. But you should know with certainty, that such a person still has the authority to baptize, to preach, and to absolve. It is not his office, but Christ's who has given it to him. If that person teaches and offers a second baptism,[3] then say: now you are stepping out of your office and stepping into your person; it is not valid. So much for this part.

"As the Father has sent me, so I send you" (John 20:21), that is, what happened to me should happen to you. He gives to them not only the same power that he himself has, but he also comforts them lest they become frightened and anxious over what the world does to them. They have Christ's example and should be certain they are sent by him. A preacher must have this confidence in his spiritual authority, if he is to preach the Gospel and forgive sins. Those who receive it from us and even we ourselves must be certain about it.

Even in the worldly estate one must be certain that he is in an approved walk of life—a prince, for example. Here, however, it is even more important, that one be sent. The text goes against the false apostles who impose themselves on the office in order to improve the world and to help the people. The text: "I send you" contradicts all this. One recognizes the false apostles in that they come strolling along, are not sent, and nothing has been commanded of them.[4] Nevertheless they boast of the Holy Spirit, want to deliver the people from their error and have mercy on their soul which is in error, and claim that the Holy Spirit drives them. Here, however, you hear that only the disciples of Jesus are driven, sent, and called to preach. Even if some folk are still so full of the Holy Spirit and even more learned, yet they do not set to work if they are not called. It is set up in this way so that I must do it. That is said to the subordinates as a warning, so that those who are not properly called are not permitted to preach. It is also commanded by the prince not to listen to such clandestine preachers;[5] for such people first take two, then ten citizens to themselves, after that the whole crowd.

It certainly pains the devil that the Word is preached so purely. For that reason I warn you if they come and want to preach—even if the pope were the preacher here and the angel Gabriel came—the angel still should not be permitted to preach. They always begin this way: that they want to save the people from error. They are commanded to be silent. If someone wants to preach and his spirit is right, then let him do as is proper: stand up and prove that you are commanded to preach. And he should not say: You do not want to listen to me! It may well be that you are more learned than our preacher; nevertheless it does not please me, for you do not do it in the right way. I also may not hit a thief on my own and hang him in my own house. Another has the right and means to punish him.

For that reason these people are poisonous worms whom the devil sends. If they were right, then they would go to the council, mayor, and pastor and say: You preach this and that, but I think this is not correct. If for this reason such people come who reject our teaching and recommend their own (as I fear that many will come) then say: It may be, we are not scorning your spirit, but use it in the right way: Christ sends his followers freely into the world with miracles; do not come and do it in some corner; otherwise I will not believe you, even if you were Gabriel. But if he still wants to preach, then demand miracles of him and confront him with this text: "I send you." Say: And if you preach the Gospel as purely as Gabriel, then you should nevertheless not preach but stand up publicly, so that others may also hear it. The Gospel is no hate-filled sermon; rather it applies to all in general. When he says: "But I will not be allowed!" You respond: "Christ would not allow it; he alone wants to be wise. If someone says something different, then one does not listen to him. So I won't listen to you." I warn you: It is no joking matter; rebellion usually follows when things happen in an disorderly manner. But if you are not permitted, then go from the city, shake the dust off the feet, as the apostles did, and let us bear our sin, though we be as evil as we want. Christ stood before Pilate and did not undermine his authority, likewise he left even Annas and Caiaphas with theirs.

The devil does not rest: there are several of them here now, as there were six years ago.[6] The devil has paraded many such preachers before me, but now they are scattered. If they can climb up into this little wooden pulpit, then we will gladly listen to their skills. But otherwise they should do as it says in the Gospel. Since you are not sent, your skills will not tear you apart. If the Holy Spirit drove me to go preach in Leipzig,[7] then I would go into no house there, but would speak to the Council or to the pastor and ask, "Would you allow me to do it?"

But thank God that the Spirit does not drive me there and my skills are not so great that I could see the Leipziger's error.[8] If they do not permit it, I do not go preach in some corner. Guard yourselves against being duped by your "spirit." These clandestine preachers are of the devil. Nobody has been raised up so openly by God's grace as we have. All these sects have raised themselves up by slithering around like snakes and thus provoking the people. We, however, are placed here in the preaching office: I, Martin Luther, am called publicly and have stood before the proper authorities. It was nothing done in a corner but a public thing. The Holy Spirit did not drive me and my brothers; rather we possess this single word for ourselves: sent! If we use that properly, the Holy Spirit is nearby.

This is all being said of the vermin,[9] so that no one gives them a hearing. If you want to be a true Christian, then say: Either be silent or, if you have the Holy Spirit, then let yourselves be sent and come in an orderly manner to this office, by which you will instruct me. If you are called, then do it; otherwise be silent, because you do not have the office of preaching and Baptism as our preacher does. If they do not permit you to say this, then take a walk. For the Holy Spirit does not preach in some corner, but publicly.

"As the Father has sent me, so I send you," that is, first with the same power, and then with the same misfortune as he himself experienced. We are to be certain of the call. That is the most glorious thing. However, thereupon it is not only a matter of using a particular authority in an orderly way for carrying out the preaching office, but also has to do with this: with what I accomplish, namely, that the Lord gives the Word of his resurrection to all preachers in their mouths and hands. Christ was sent to deliver lost souls and so were the apostles. Paul boasts (2 Corinthians 13:10) that he has the power, given him by the Lord, for building up and not tearing down.

If only our bishops believed that! No doubt they have been sent, and they hold their office legitimately—that we cannot deny. But they do not act as Christ and their office demand. They should be simple deliverers, saviors, and Christs, for he has not come to destroy souls, but to save them.

But take a look at what kind of people the bishops are: They govern Christianity with mere laws. But if it is only ruled with new laws about foods, vows, and clothes, then it is perverted. The office of Christianity is to preach the forgiveness of sins and to indicate to the world that it is saved through Christ and loosed from sins and set free from all laws.

The Gospel liberates from laws, but they do nothing other than to bind us with their self-concocted laws and ropes. Even the pope does nothing else. He does it in this way: He forgives the sins of those who trespass against his own laws. That is how he becomes antichrist, who erects a new law and a new forgiveness of sins instead of the evangelical forgiveness by which we become free from all laws (2 Thessalonians 2:4). He has made ropes for us and bound us, and yet he is supposed to set us free. Here the wolf is preaching in the sheep fold. Yesterday you heard that a Christian is over every law,[10] but they burden Christianity with so many ropes.

The authority of the pope is a devilish authority, which entangles us so—especially in the conscience. To be sure, the emperor attaches ropes to our hands and feet, to our body and goods, and to whatever we possess. That is outwardly proper, would be fine, and is to be tolerated. The pope, however, puts laws and ropes on the conscience.

This means he is not sent as Christ was sent. They are indeed called and sent by God but not in the manner of Christ, who was sent to be a redeemer, who gives peace to the human conscience, and does not to entangle the people with law. With the pope, however, it is reversed: He burdens, confuses, and frightens the people, as formerly all kings were frightened before the pope's command; for his office was only his own wantonness. So the pope has abused the Holy Spirit's office for his person, although it was established to be used for others, to forgive and retain the sins of others, to comfort the afflicted, and to frighten the impenitent, even if they fast themselves to death.

So the Christian office exists for this: to forgive sins.[11] If they would pay attention to this, then they would have to recognize that we are set in this office to make the people righteous through the Gospel and the forgiveness of sins.

So you have it in this word that you are not justified by your works or your good life but through the mouth of your pastor who should speak to you a word so that your holiness is based on the Word which Christ has given his apostles. Then you will be safe and will not die. He has thereby torn away all positions of righteousness and holiness and by this text shown the forgiveness of sins to the people. All orders and monasteries are thereby abolished. For if someone claims to have the forgiveness of sins through his particular walk of life, then the devil is in there. Here, however, all that is cut off. Here it says: Encourage a person with a friendly word. That should count for more than all orders.

That is what this text intends: "As the Father has sent me, so I send you," namely, so that the people become righteous. How? Through the Gospel, not through laws. If you speak a word over them by your mouth, then they become righteous. If you want to make them righteous, then say: "your sins are forgiven." Such power does not come from the power of the pope, but from the Word of Christ which he has put in the mouth of every preacher. So this text is to be regarded as glorious, and it goes beyond all teaching about works and beyond the imperial eagle.[12]

Endnotes

[1] On the Donatists, see above, p. 77 note 10.
[2] Luther's own daughter, Elizabeth, had been born in December 1527.
[3] A reference to the Anabaptists who disparaged infant Baptism.

[4] With John 20:22 as his text, Luther expanded on this idea in a sermon preached on 27 April 1522. See Lenker 2:376.

[5] German: *Winkelprediger:* Anabaptist preachers who speak in some hidden corner because they have no call.

[6] Luther is thinking of the Zwickau prophets, who had shown up in Wittenberg during his absence at the Wartburg in 1521, and Karlstadt, who from 1521–22 had tried to take over Luther's preaching post at St. Mary's church in Wittenberg without proper authorization.

[7] Unlikely at the time, since it was controlled by Luther's archenemy, Duke George of Saxony. Shortly after George's death, he first preached there on Pentecost 1540 at the invitation of the new prince and the city council.

[8] An ironical statement, imitating the claims of the *Winkelprediger.*

[9] Luther here makes a play on words: the words "vermin" and "shitters" differ by only one letter in German.

[10] See above, p. 185f.

[11] The following year, in the Augsburg Confession, article XXVIII, the same point is made.

[12] Either: over all imperial laws, or: over imperial commands to crush the evangelicals.

Easter Tuesday Afternoon
March 30, 1529
The Purpose of Christ's Resurrection: Repentance and Forgiveness of Sin
(Luke 24:45–47)

This morning we heard how Christ sent his disciples into the world and installed them in their office to forgive and retain sins. Thus he makes this out of the preaching office: that our life and all that we are consists in this office. For it is written that preachers carry in their mouths the Word of God that brings death and proclaims life. For one must not regard these words as unimportant. Paul praises the phrase, "the forgiveness of sins," in all his epistles. The preaching office and the Gospel are such wonderful things to him that it is a miracle, and he calls the preaching office "the ministry of reconciliation" (2 Corinthians 5:18) because Christ has committed to them the office which takes away death and sin and settles and puts all things right. Satan knows this well.

For this reason he has done so much so that this office may not remain pure. Therefore the fanatics propose something else when reconciliation and forgiveness of sins is preached, namely, laws which, like the pope's or the bishop's authority, are external. And they imagine this is something great. There, too, the "religious"[1] came and made their laws about their vows. But Christ does not ask about whether you eat this or that, whether you wear a cowl or some other garment. These things are of no importance; instead be a mediator, a purveyor, and forgiver of sins so that you take the sins from the people and destroy death and sin. This is my command, says Christ, that through your office the people are set free from sin.

Now the text continues with a section where he expresses this even more clearly: "Thus it is written that the Christ had to suffer and to rise from the dead on the third day, and that repentance and forgiveness of sins is to be proclaimed in his name" (Luke 24:46f.). In this text you have again what I have been preaching these past few days. "Christ had to." In this way and no other. What need is there to want to produce many other teachings and states? "Thus it is written," that is to say, it did not happen in any old which way, that I and not another should die, but "Christ had to suffer and to rise on the third day, and repentance and forgiveness of sins is to be proclaimed in his name." If repentance and forgiveness of sins is to come, then it would have to happen in this way, that I, Christ, died and rose.

This is certainly a powerful text. With clear words he emphasizes his suffering, and for this reason we also emphasize its goal and fruit so that repentance and forgiveness of sin is preached. It is as if he were saying: Without this, had I not died and risen, there would be no repentance and forgiveness of sins. Judas and Cain also repented. But what was the result? Cain said, "My sin is greater than what can be forgiven me" (cf. Genesis 4:13), and Judas said, "I have sinned by betraying innocent blood" (Matthew 27:4).

That was a repentance that grew from one's own meditation without the Gospel of the Lord's death and resurrection, which proclaims to you that your sins are so great Christ had to die for them. That is a "gallows remorse,"[2] despair, but not repentance; a "Judas repentance" because repentance and forgiveness of sins are not connected to it. Apart from the Gospel no repentance avails, but only hurts a person.

If I get letters of indulgence, and the pope gives absolution from his authority and does not apply the Gospel to me, then it is nothing, for it stands apart from faith and I do not hear God's Word. Thus the pope writes in his letters, "I absolve you according to my apostolic authority," and has sucked everything into his own authority and made it more a prayer than a declaration when he also writes in that very place: "May God have mercy on you!" Instead the preacher must conclude by saying: Christ, God, says this to you! In this lies the truth. Trust in it! But it has nothing to do with the authority of the apostles or the bishops.

True absolution should happen in Jesus' name, however humble the preacher is. Look only at the words! "Christ had to suffer and die." The Scripture would be fulfilled that there is no repentance or forgiveness of sins apart from Christ. Those who diligently study the Scripture understand this. In the Scripture it says, "I will put enmity between you and the woman, between your offspring and hers; he will strike your head, and you will strike his heel" (Genesis 3:15).[3] There Adam received repentance and forgiveness of sins in the name of Christ who was to fight with sin, death, and the devil. Whoever preaches differently makes a serious error. Christ had to suffer. That was one part.

But he was not to remain in death. He has taken it upon himself with the Passion and then with his resurrection he has conquered. And this Passion and resurrection must be grasped through the office of preaching: Otherwise no one would experience and know it. The external word reveals it, for Christ "opened their minds to understand the Scripture." "Therefore Christ had to suffer," etc. But it is not supposed to remain there but is to be preached about and announced to the people.

For this reason it is a fine word: "Repentance and forgiveness of sins is to be proclaimed in his name." Repentance should not be preached in the name of Judas, Cain, the Carthusians, Augustine,

Bernard, or Francis:[4] Away with them! Your repentance and your life must not bear the name of the one who is performing it—otherwise it is a "Cain's repentance." Why? If repentance is preached apart from the name of Christ, then it is preached in our name. A person who repents in the name of the Carthusians thinks: With this or that work you will atone for sin. That repentance is in the name of the Carthusians, for they have the name and the work, just as each artisan gets his name from his work.

Satan loves that repentance. For he well knows what end it serves, namely, that in the end a person despairs. Repentance must be something higher, namely, in the name of Christ. It must be a repentance that does not occur through our work or remorse over our own deeds, as when Judas saw the work he had done and wanted to repent. But remorse and repentance in Jesus' name goes beyond all good and evil works.

Repentance is the same for the greatest saint as for the greatest sinner. We can do whatever we want, but in this life there is only a condemned existence. But no one wants to hear about such a repentance, even though it is the repentance Christ desires, namely, that we all must say: "I am a sinner." But there comes Caiaphas and Annas with all saints who say, "God, I thank you that I am not like other people: thieves, rogues, adulterers, or even like this tax collector. I fast twice a week; I give a tenth of my income" (Luke 18:11f.), as the Pharisee said. But Christ desires to create a repentance that exceeds all these: All who are apart from me are condemned, and whoever does not confess being a sinner is lost.

So you should indeed say: "If I have done everything as best as I can, I am still an unworthy servant (Luke 17:10) because even before I do it, I am guilty one hundred times over before God." When all is said and done, if you have kept the 10 Commandments, you do not thereby earn heaven. Or what have you given to the Lord God for him to give you body and soul and all their faculties? If he wanted to keep accounts with you, then you are ten times more indebted to God for that which he has given you. Therefore you still have nothing over against heaven. If you are to have something more, then something higher must come. Therefore acknowledge that everything is sin and you are worthy of condemnation.

The Lord is talking about this kind of repentance. With it a person will not easily fall into the "Judas repentance," for it is a saving repentance that flows from Christ. The godless stumble on to a single sin, and, if they are able to make satisfaction for it, they think, that's enough. This is a beggarly and partial repentance. But Christian repentance consists of this, that a person believes that everything is sin. Hence it follows that there is no satisfaction. Repentance according to the Holy Scripture is a repentance without satisfaction.[5] First of all, it is necessary that I acknowledge my error and my sin and treat it as my enemy, but I also acknowledge that I can make no satisfaction for it. For if everything is sin, then even the works with which I want to make satisfaction are sin.

Therefore when this word repentance is preached in Jesus' name, it sets aside that repentance defined in the law books of the pope; for before God, all good works are sins. In conclusion I must say: My works don't do it. That is the first thing that is preached to the world, namely, that it is able to do nothing. If it confesses this, then it is in this repentance. Where not, then it is in the "Judas repentance" and does not want to receive a complete repentance but only a partial one, as the saints who depend on works have a beggarly and partial satisfaction for one sin, but do not acknowledge the other sins.

But that is not a sermon for the common rabble. Still, because we have opportunity, we must speak of these most Christian things so that Christians make a distinction between faith and works. Repentance is a complete repentance without works. That is: I believe it when Jesus Christ calls me a sinner, and, I believe that everything in me is condemned, and I confess as much. But such repentance cannot happen without faith. Reason does not believe it because it thinks we still have something good in us. True repentance begins with faith in the name of the Lord. There one does not despair because it is not a Judas repentance but flows from the Word, which says it is all sin. This faith stands firm and remains standing and has an advantage for this reason: Forgiveness of sins follows it.

If Christ had wanted to speak after the manner of the pope, then he would have said, "Repentance and satisfaction for sins." But he says, "Repentance and forgiveness of sins," that is, that the sin be acknowledged and forgiven. The world does not know these two parts, and the papists do not teach one to acknowledge sin. But to preach repentance means to teach a proper knowledge of sin and to point to Christ. Therefore, bring it together as Christ does: "Therefore Christ had to suffer and rise and rise from the dead on the third day, and that repentance and forgiveness of sins is to be proclaimed in his name." If you bring them together, then repentance and forgiveness of sins are pure thunderbolts against that hypocritical repentance which consists in satisfaction through works.

To be sure we had repentance in the political sphere and in the papacy. But true repentance is preached in the name of the Lord who suffered and is risen from the dead. His suffering, death and resurrection should give this, that a person may acknowledge sins and their forgiveness. If Christ had not died, we would know nothing of this repentance and forgiveness of sins. All who depend on works righteousness preach repentance in their own name and despair. For this reason the Lord says his work has taken place so that it would be preached to us and bring us to the knowledge of sin; then immediately forgiveness follows right on its heels.

For this reason in Christianity sorrow for sin and satisfaction avail nothing for sins, but only the pure knowledge of sin and the certain promise that the sins are forgiven. Apart from Christ there is no knowledge of sin, to say nothing of forgiveness, because they do not believe that Christ has died for them and say, "I have taken up these holy orders so that I have no need of Christ. I know of no sin. If I do commit sin, then I can do penance with my works." Then Christ is superfluous. But if those who hear the Word (which is preached in his name and which calls everyone a sinner even if they are the most holy) believe it, then their sins are forgiven; if they do not believe, then they are not forgiven. Whoever does not want to be a sinner scrape and scratch out the little words "repentance" and "forgiveness of sins" and do not listen to this sermon! These words are placed here so excellently. With these words Christ soars above all holiness based on the law.

"To all nations." There no one is excluded; it is true for all: Mend your ways! The world says: But how? I feel no sin. I cannot believe such words! Answer in this way: If your sins do not bite you, then may the Word bite you! Say: Who knows one's own sin? I believe your Word that I am a sinner!" If that is true, then you are forgiven if only you seriously acknowledge yourself as a sinner.

Now what the forgiveness of sins brings with it you have often heard: it is sheer grace; it is a gift, it is not a merit. For if something is given, it is not earned; it is not attained through all the good works and merits in the world. But nevertheless repentance and forgiveness of sins, which are opposed to each other, are bound to one another. How do you reconcile that? Not in the papacy, because there one says: "Repentance is satisfaction for sins." That does not accord with forgiveness. For this reason they do not tolerate one another. This has happened because they have defined repentance like the worldly authority, where a judge punishes a thief by making him pay the penalty.

But if a person makes satisfaction for his sins, it is not repentance in the Gospel but only here on earth. Rather in the Gospel repentance consists of acknowledging and believing that we are sinners who can never repent. It is a confession and acknowledgement of sin as Paul says, "for through the law comes the knowledge of sin" (Romans 3:20). So when he says: "all have sinned" (Romans 3:23), I say: "Yes, Lord, I believe it even if I do not feel it." Repentance is the knowledge of sin from God's Word, which says we are all sinners. This repentance does not fight against the forgiveness of sins because it acknowledges sin, as Psalm 51:4 says, "Against you, you alone, have I sinned and done what is evil in your sight, so that you are justified in your sentence and blameless when you pass judgment."

The true meaning of these words is knowing that repentance is acknowledgment and confession of sins, that all is lost and there is no other means and counsel against sin than this: forgiveness. So a Christian arrives nicely at true repentance.

Then we must learn to speak about righteousness and truth differently than the pope and the world. They also speak about them and say: Righteousness is when I try to give to others what is due them. Sure, leave me alone and try to give to the Lord what is due to him![6] On the contrary, the Scripture calls righteousness something else, namely, faith in Christ. It is not reason but the Word that says this. Reason says: Do penance! Yes, when you have sinned you must also do penance by being punished. Then the pope says: "Because that's the way it is in the world, it is the same in the Gospel."

But repentance consists of acknowledging everything that is mine is sin. You will never acknowledge this by using reason. But Christ commands that repentance be preached in his name: "So that you are justified in your sentence and blameless when you pass judgment." This is repentance, and at the same time you have the forgiveness of sins, because you acknowledge your sins and you are a true Jew[7] and confess according to the Word of God that everything is sin. This is not according to reason, which says: "If I perform external righteousness, then it is not sin."

To be sure, that is indeed a worldly righteousness, yet before God it does not matter, because here repentance and forgiveness of sins are preached in his name. The executioner does not allow sin to be repented for in this way. If a person has confessed a sin, he says, "Hold out your head!" But here when a person has confessed a sin, he or she should know no other satisfaction than forgiveness of sins. Christian satisfaction is nothing other than forgiveness. Christ, his suffering, and his resurrection have accomplished it. You are forgiven for his sake.

But the Roman church scoffs at this. It demands a worldly satisfaction, which does not avail in the Gospel. In the Gospel, satisfaction is nothing but the forgiveness of sins, so that a Christian may learn: Satisfaction is the forgiveness of sins. But it is driven home to us by the rod of the parents and school masters that if one is aware of sin, then there is punishment. And from this the Christian church and authority have learned to apply feeling and experience: Where sin is, there satisfaction should be.

For this reason it is indeed necessary that one should confess: I am a sinner. But one must proceed carefully so that one does not permit a worldly repentance, lest I deny Christ. But if you are aware of your sins, you are precisely in the place where Christ commands that repentance be preached in his name. If you believe everything is sin, then believe that everything is forgiven. The two should not be separated. Both are given to you: knowledge of sins and forgiveness of sin. Therefore the greater emphasis lies in the forgiveness of sins through Christ's suffering and resurrection. My works do not accomplish it, for then I would have to deny Christ. If you want to make satisfaction, then you do not need the forgiveness of sins and something better than Christ and God! Then let the devil help you!

Judas dealt with his repentance according to reason and did not grasp the statement that repentance and forgiveness of sins should be preached in Christ's name. Our adversaries do not tolerate this teaching, but say: Some things are sin, some are not. We want to make satisfaction with the one for the other. At the same time such people thereby destroy the suffering of Christ and his resurrection. Such penalty and penance must not enter into the Gospel. Instead, true repentance must be preached throughout the entire world.

Thus we have now spoken about the resurrection of Christ and what its purpose is.

Endnotes

[1] German: *Geistliche*: spirituals, a common term for monks, nuns, and friars.

[2] Remorse in the face of certain punishment.

[3] Following the exegetical tradition, Luther here interprets this text as the first Gospel and promise of Christ to Adam and Eve.

[4] The last three names refer to important figures for the Augustinian, Cistercian, and Franciscan orders.

[5] In the *Instructions for the Visitors of Parish Pastors in Electoral Saxony* of 1528 (LW 40:293–97), Luther and Melanchthon reject satisfaction, the third part of the medieval sacrament of Penance (along with contrition and confession). They also redefine the first two along the lines of Law and Gospel.

[6] Here Luther attacks the use of the philosophical definition of righteousness, derived from Aristotle and Cicero, in interpreting the Gospel. This definition survives in the English sayings, "To each his own" and "just desserts." Luther's rejection of this definition is part and parcel of his so-called Reformation breakthrough, in which he interpreted Romans 1:17 not according to active righteousness (where God gives each person his or her "just desserts") but a passive righteousness (whereby God declares each to be righteous through the righteousness of another, Christ, in faith). See LW 31:336–38.

[7] See above, p. 167 note 1.

Easter Wednesday Morning
March 31, 1529
The Resurrection of the Body
(1 Corinthians 15:1ff.)

In these days of Easter we have hardly made reference to the matter of the resurrection because the material is too profuse. First of all, you have heard that one must believe Christ is risen according to the story and that this avails for us, that we rise from sins and become free of all sins, and that the soul rises. But how a person is to rise bodily, we have not yet touched upon. But now we want to consider what the Apostles' Creed says. And we want to take up St. Paul, who says to the Corinthians: "Now I would remind you, brothers and sisters, of the gospel that I have proclaimed to you" (1 Corinthians 15:1).

Here the apostle clearly acts as if the entire Gospel were nothing other than the resurrection of Christ! Therefore he insists on this article in his preaching. The apostle emphasized no other article so relentlessly. This is also necessary for us because Satan wants to divert us from this article and poses strange questions. Therefore Paul says, "So we have proclaimed and so you have come to believe" (v. 11). But you want to come with all sorts of questions and thereby lose both Christ's suffering and his resurrection.

"Now if Christ is proclaimed as raised from the dead, how can some of you say that there is no resurrection of the dead?" (v. 12). Those people were St. Paul's dear children and students, who had embraced the preaching of the Gospel and who now had fallen into all kinds of errors. He states there are some among you who say: Christ is dead. If he is dead then he is dead and never appears again. This is what the Corinthians were doing.

Then it should come as no surprise when the same thing also happens among us. The apostle confirmed this teaching with miracles and demonstration of the Holy Spirit. And yet already during his lifetime his opponents began to make a mockery of it. Of necessity other errors must also follow. If one does not hold to the article of the resurrection of Christ as one should hold it, all other articles of faith are lost.

For this reason there is even today a great lacking of faith in this article, so that there are only a few who believe the article of the resurrection of the body. Especially in Italy and among the nobility and big shots it is a ridiculous sermon that there should be a resurrection of the dead, and they mock: "Do you think that one fellow is hiding in another? Don't you think when you have died that the soul leaves the body like a pea from a pod?"[1] But we believe in the resurrection of the body. Flesh means the physical body. "The Word became flesh" (John 1:14), that is: A person is a being who has a living body which no one has unless body and soul are bound together.

We believe that these two will come together again. That is difficult to believe because reason looks at the work, and the eyes see that the body has been covered with dirt. And there is no more filthy and smelly carcass than that of a dead person. Thus I have to say: The one is burned, the other is torn to pieces; here one leaves an arm, there a bone. If you want to measure it using reason, then you lose the resurrection of the dead. Then such strange ideas come along that one says: There is nothing to the resurrection of the dead. Such things happen in all parts of Christian teaching. As with sins: If you consider them, then you certainly depart from the forgiveness of sins. If you want to see whether it makes sense or not to reason, then it is too late. So it goes with the fanatical spirits who say: Bread is bread, how can bread be body? Water is water, how can water bathe the soul and give it eternal life? That is impossible!

For this reason this is the skill which Paul teaches them and calls them back to the sermon: "So we proclaim and so you have come to believe" (v. 11). If one will not allow it to remain in the Word, then it is impossible for reason to believe something. For it is against the experience and perception of reason, so that reason cannot grasp it. Reason sees one rotting on the cross and the worms eating and thinks: Is he supposed to rise? Then he should certainly not perish shamefully as any other living creature does. One consumes other wild animals; people are buried among the worms. It is easier to believe that all birds rise than it is that people rise. It is the same also with sins. Our conscience is so struck by the experience of sin that when I speak of the forgiveness of sins, the conscience responds: My heart says something quite different.

If you want to judge as you perceive and see, then we have lost it. Then the sermon is not in your heart but in your reason which meditates on the articles of faith. If you do not want to believe that the Word is worth more than what your eyes see and your feelings perceive, then you are done for. For this reason the resurrection of the dead is an article that one must believe. I do not perceive that Christ is raised, but the Word says it. I feel the sin but the Word says those who believe are forgiven. But I do not see the faith! I see that Christians die like all others. But the Word says that they rise.

Therefore one may not judge according to perception and sight but according to the Word. There is nothing greater than what the evangelical preachers have in their mouths: You are a lord over Satan, devil and hell. Our opponents say, This is pure nonsense. For they see in us the opposite, namely, that we are in the power of the devil and sin. For this reason, they judge according to what is in front of their eyes. But we preach that I am a lord over the devil and yet I feel that I am under him. The one thing must be felt, the other must be believed. Perception is to follow after faith, not precede it. Satan sets himself against me with all his tyrants and fanatics, who are much stronger than we are, and yet the Gospel wants us to believe differently than what we see and feel, namely, that although I feel the devil is my lord, I believe that he is my servant and therefore I conquer and subjugate him.

Therefore the fanatical spirits are defeated by the very fact that they are over me. I do not see that, but I believe that. It is the same way with this, that although I feel the sin and a conscience burdened with sin, I am a victor over sin not in feeling but in the Word. Death is also defeated in the same way. But, you say, it still comes with pestilence, or the executioner burns or drowns me! There you are a fine lord over death! Answer: I am the one according to feeling, the other according to faith! Therefore those who are buried smell and are devoured, and yet they are much more lovely than the stars of heaven. The one I see, the other not. Yet it must even be so with Christ. Certainly it was difficult for the Jews to believe that Christ, who lay in the sealed tomb, should be a lord over death while lying imprisoned under death. Nevertheless, Paul says, both are true.

For this reason I often say to the many who want to follow reason: Protect yourself from the "Why?" and from meditation. Eve fell into all kinds of temptation for this reason, namely, on account of the "Why?" And when you get mixed up with the "Why?" you are lost just as surely as Eve. But you are in paradise if you do not listen to the "Why?" but instead cling to the Word. Through the "Why?" a great number have allowed themselves to be drawn far from the Word. St. Paul complains that the Corinthians are beginning to say the resurrection is nothing. Because this is their saying and prattle, not his preaching, then they must be wrong.

If this article is to be maintained, then one must cling to the Word. For this reason Paul says here: "Now I would remind you, brothers and sisters, of the good news that I have proclaimed to you, which you in turn received, in which also you stand" (1 Corinthians 15:1). You have accepted the Gospel; in this you stand and in this you will be saved. There he moves them completely away from their "Why?" and wants to direct them toward his Gospel. If you will stand and not be overthrown, then you stand only in the Gospel. He bestows the power to resist Satan on no other thing than the Gospel. Whoever does not have the Gospel or lets it be perverted never stands. For this reason the devil is a professional soldier,[2] and for this reason he is intent on one thing: to snatch the Word away. Then he has us where he wants. For this reason he seizes it through the fanatics and sects and through our troubled thoughts in the heart. For the Gospel alone is such a difficult burden for him that he cannot endure it.

For this reason the Apostle says in the following verses: We preach that Christ is risen "in accordance with the Scripture" (v. 3). He repeatedly hammers away at this, and not without reason. For there is no permanence in our faith, unless the bodily, oral Word sticks in our hearts. The Scripture is not only a written thing. The Enthusiasts call it a letter that gives no life. And even if it gave no life, this text here still says that we should stick to the Scripture or we will lose Christ. We preach Christ not according to reason, not according to the wisdom of the world or human wisdom, not according to human laws and commands, not according to one's own thoughts, but "in accordance with the Scripture," which should be a witness in our hearts against all the objections of reason.

For this reason a Christian says: This one has died from the plague and smells.[3] Yet there the sun goes out, and a body more beautiful than the sun goes into the earth. But I do not see it. True, but "in accordance with the Scripture." Reason does not grasp that in a stinking body a new life lies hidden like a sun. Cling to the Scripture alone which fosters this faith. In the same way with Christ. He laid in the tomb, but "on the third day" he was seen. Consider, Paul says, what you have heard and what is preached to you. There you will stand—if you stick to the Gospel that you have received—and you will be saved. And you know, "in what manner I have proclaimed it to you."

See how sharply he warns and threatens them at the same time. There was nothing lacking in the sermon. If something is lacking, then it is our fault. If you have not kept it, then "your faith has been in vain." Who may venture to say such? Paul speaks not about keeping the commandments, but the Gospel. If you have not kept this "your faith has been in vain." As if to say: I have not preached in such a manner that you talk about the resurrection according to reason. That is preaching about the dead in the manner common people and the world speak. If you lose the manner in which I have preached, then you have also lost the faith. For this is the way of the world, which has surrendered the faith. Just so, too, you have lost everything.

But this is the greatest comfort, that Christians already stand in eternal life in so far as they look to the Word. In this they see their life, as in the article, "I believe in the resurrection of the body." They have it already in their body, except that it is still in the future. Certainly this eternal life will make them abhor the present life, so that they desire and hope for the future life. But if the converse is true, then they are worldly persons.

If I am to believe this—that when I am a Christian, I may live and may look at death as a nothing even though it kills us—then faith and the Word are necessary, but not reason. And one must think that the Word is not a human dream, but God's Word. Christ, who has died in such shame and disgrace, is risen. No one else has ever died such a despairing death; for his enemies lay above and his odor smelled to high heaven as it is when our bodies pollute the air with their stench. And yet he proved that the Scripture is true.

But here there is no reason or wisdom; they have not understood the faintest glimmer of these things. According to these words Christ had to remain living in the tomb. Therefore it will also happen with us: We will rot, but the Word is living and in that we are as bright as the sun. In the tomb, in the plague, I do not see life, but only in these words: "I believe in the resurrection of the body" and then as follows in our text: If Christ is risen, then we will also rise (1 Corinthians 15:20).

The one statement implies the other. But if I believe weakly, how should I proceed? Then I know, I am a lord over all fanatics and the devil, indeed not according to my feelings, but in faith. "The greater will serve the lesser" (Genesis 25:23). The one who has the Word is over all, so "that he might learn that godliness is more powerful than anything" (Wisdom of Solomon 10:12). But this we could not grasp because of the weakness, for we feel the opposite about it. Then I feel the sin and become weak. I have to have a pure conscience and yet my heart is bound.

According to my feelings it is vastly different, for Satan, flesh, and world torment me sorely. If it were a matter of feeling, all would be lost. But precisely when I feel how sin burdens me, I am a lord over sin because Christ has died for me. When I see him dying, there pure weakness is to be seen. The word of Scripture is weak, and the plague, cross, and sword carry away the entire world. But although I am still so weak, if I only cling to the Word, I break through all these afflictions, and the Scripture will remain standing.

That indeed is our struggle. For this reason faith is not an idea, but a valiant hero who is to hold bravely to the words, "I believe in the resurrection of the body." This Word is nevertheless such a power to tear apart heaven and earth and to open up all graves. Reason says: There is no resurrection. But the Word can and will do it. Paul says, all who abide in this Word will be saved (v. 2). No matter how weak they are because of plague and death, yet they will live because of the Scripture, not because of feeling.

Satan has always placed himself over against the Scripture but can do nothing. As long as the word of the resurrection is in you, he does nothing to you, as the Scripture says, "[God] gave him victory in the arduous contest so that he might learn that godliness is more powerful than anything" (Wisdom of Solomon 10:12). No one knows how powerful the Word is—not only in the strife and wavering, but also in that it can preserve a person in the truth from all error. If you do not cling to the Word alone, then you will knock down everything. There is no other defense against such blows except the Word alone. The fanatics do not believe that, and they go around with "enthusiastic" ideas. There is no comfort for them when they do not leave their own thoughts. I can only be comforted through the Word: Christ has died and is risen. If the Word does not do it, then you are lost.

There is no other way in which you can be comforted. We must stick to the Gospel that we have received. If Christ had had another way to comfort us than through the Gospel, then Paul would have pointed it out to us. It costs no money nor effort, only that the heart says Yes. Otherwise it cannot be of help. But if the heart believes in him, then it can oppose all devils and the world. Even when a little child is weak, the mother will not throw it away because it is stinking and weak, mangy and lost. But if the child escapes the mother's care, then it is all over with it, then the lice will eat you. But one certainly sees clearly in our age that this article is not believed. In Italy it is actually denied and it is made fun of. The word of the resurrection must be emphasized.

Let this be enough at this time to begin speaking of this matter.

Endnotes

[1] Luther is here caricaturing the beliefs of the Italian Platonists, such as Pico della Mirandola (1463–1494), who held to the transmigration of souls, as did Plato.

[2] German: *Junker:* a nobleman who was required to fight for his lord.

[3] The plague had most recently ravaged Wittenberg in 1527. Luther and Bugenhagen, as the city's pastors, had remained in town to comfort the sick and grieving, to bury the dead, and to support the survivors. See LW 43:113–38.

www.ingramcontent.com/pod-product-compliance
Lightning Source LLC
Chambersburg PA
CBHW021811220426
43662CB00006B/268